THE GREAT CLIPPERS

Jane D. Lyon

AMERICAN HERITAGE • NEW WORD CITY

Published by New Word City, Inc.

For more information about New Word City, visit our Web site at
NewWordCity.com

INTRODUCTION

This book documents the crowning achievement of men whose contribution to the early growth of the United States probably exceeded that of any other group of comparable numbers.

American mariner-merchants had already accomplished the impossible. Against fantastic odds, they had built a fleet that proved one of the decisive factors in the American Revolution and the War of 1812. They had gathered the wealth that founded the first banks in the United States and built its first railroads, factories, and steamships. They had paid the duties that alone enabled Thomas Jefferson to purchase the vast Louisiana territory. They had made the U.S. merchant marine superior in quality to any other afloat. Now, they were to cap their achievements by making it equally superior in size, and in the process, producing the greatest, swiftest, and most beautiful craft the world had ever seen - the clipper ship.

This study not only traces the origins, development, and achievements of the clipper, but enlivens the dry bones of historic fact with flesh and blood. A great era comes to life as captain and crew pace the broad, slowly heaving decks and towering pyramids of canvas heel and sway overhead. Great three-deckers race home from Melbourne or Hong Kong, straining canvas piled tier on tier. Crews face killing hardships in the Cape Horn passage and week-long gales that strip the ship to bare poles, reducing them to a handful of stricken, hobbling creatures.

The clippers were the flowering of fifty centuries of a harsh and dangerous mode of life, and like all flowers their reign was brief. The wealth that had fostered economic and industrial advance brought with it a demand for faster and more dependable transportation, and steam was the answer.

1
PRELUDE TO GLORY

I n the early days of the United States, the sea offered young Americans a glamorous and exciting way of life. Many lived within sight of salt water, most could sniff it, and everyone's life was affected in some way, large or small, by the sea and its ships and the men who manned them.

From an uncle just off a whaler, an older brother home from the Mediterranean, or a cousin back from China, young men heard tales of hair-raising escapes from pirates, of lovely women on flower-scented islands, of fierce head-hunting cannibals, of strange lands and exotic customs. They smelled spices and pepper from the East, tasted yellow lemons from Spain, drank China tea or South American coffee, and fingered the silks and nankeens brought home from the Orient. And, their minds fired with the color and glamor of far-off lands, they went to sea, not only for adventure and to see the world, but to carve out a career. For if the ambition was to become a captain, there was both money and prestige in such a goal.

There was something else, too, that pulled people to sea. A patriotism had grown from the tales of derring-do: tales of colonists turned smugglers to avoid unjust British taxes, or of Revolutionary War privateers, swift craft that preyed on British merchant ships. After the Revolution, there was the urge to show the world that America was as good as anybody else on the high seas - and maybe even better.

Sometimes it seemed as if there were not enough ships to take care of all those who wanted to go to sea. When Captain Daniel Bacon of Barnstable, Massachusetts, came home from China in 1811, half the boys in town wanted to sign on for his next voyage. And when salty breezes reached back into the country, farm children forsook their chores and headed for the salt water and its brave promise.

The youngsters who lived along the coast had the advantage over their country cousins. They grew up knowing how to tell a schooner from a sloop or the difference between square-rigged and fore-and-aft-rigged. Naming the sails of a ship was like breathing - they did not have to think about it.

One such youngster was Nathaniel Brown Palmer, born in 1799 in the bustling seaport of Stonington, Connecticut. Nat's father was a shipbuilder. From the time he could crawl, Nat's playground was his father's shipyard and his toys the chips and sawdust in the yard. His earliest teachers were shipwrights and riggers and sailmakers, and he learned what made a dull sailer and why, given two hulls of equal tonnage, the longer would likely sail faster. He soaked up the yarns the sailors spun as they waited for their ships to be repaired. He learned how to swim and how to handle his own small sailboat.

On top of all this, young Nat sat bug-eyed on the edge of a front-row seat, watching the thrilling drama of blockade-running during the War of 1812. The harbor at Stonington was always crowded with fleet coasters waiting for a chance to run the British blockade. Often, when a fog lifted, a blockade-runner would be found right under the guns of the British, and her crew would pile on sail and streak for Stonington with cannon balls whistling behind them and cheers of encouragement from the shore ahead.

What child would not have yearned to be one of such a crew? At fourteen, Nat Palmer signed on as an apprentice seaman.

A blockade-runner was the best school that he could have chosen, for the skippers of these coasters were superb navigators. The crews boasted of their captains that they "could smell their way through fog by night from Hell Gate to Providence with their eyes shut." For four years, during the war and after, Palmer sailed on sloops and schooners, advancing to seaman, to mate, and finally, at the ripe old age of eighteen, to master of the *Galena,* a small schooner.

For the times, this youthful career was not unusual since schooling stopped at fourteen or fifteen. If going to sea, most sailors set their hearts on a command, and each, in rising to the top, made way for others. A story is told of the crew of one brigantine, thirteen in all, each of whom ended as master of a vessel, some before they were old enough to vote.

When Nat was nineteen, he joined the crew of the *Hersilia* in a search for new sealing grounds. The skins of the fur seal were so valuable that a single shipload of them meant a profit of thousands of dollars. Guided by Palmer, the *Hersilia* nosed into a new breeding ground in the South Shetland Islands, near the South Pole, and came home with a cargo of skins worth $20,000. The next year, when a fleet of sealers put out from Stonington, Nat, only twenty-one, was in command of the *Hero,* a fifty-foot sloop that served the fleet as scout.

On this voyage, Palmer found more than seal rookeries. In 1820, he sighted a vast peninsula of Antarctica that is still often called Palmer Land.

Sometime later, Palmer undertook to supply arms and ammunition to Simón Bolívar, the Great Liberator, who was freeing South America from Spanish rule. Palmer had filled out now and was a burly, square-shouldered man of authority. On these dangerous voyages, he won the reputation that made him famous in the clipper era - he was a driver who pushed his ships faster than most captains would have considered prudent. Pirates still infested Caribbean waters, and speed was the best weapon against them.

In 1833, Palmer was made captain of a packet, the ship that was the immediate forerunner of the clipper. It was a command for which he was superbly fitted; all of his special talents would now be put to use.

With the end of the War of 1812, American ships were at last able to sail the seas without threats from foreign privateers. Trade was carried on by tramp ships that went from port to port picking up whatever cargoes they could, and by regular traders that sailed only between one port and another, at no set date.

Most so-called regular traders were on the North Atlantic run, sailing between England or Europe and America. They made one round trip in the spring and one in the fall, shunning the dangers of the wintertime passage. A sailing date was usually announced, but there were always delays. No ship would sail until holds were fully freighted and the weather was fair. Passengers cooled their heels for days, while their tempers grew hot.

If these delays vexed the passengers, they cost the merchants good money. The longer their goods were delayed, the longer it took to get paid for them. And so, in 1817, some New York merchants clubbed together and announced a regularly scheduled service for passengers, mail, and freight between New York and Liverpool. These ships would sail rain or shine, gale or calm, full or empty, at a definite time once a month, and would be known as the Black Ball Line.

The first packet ship was to sail from New York at 10 a.m., January 5, 1818, but no one believed it would. Snow was falling as a crowd gathered at an East River wharf to jeer. But when the tide turned and the church bells rang out the hour, a mail bag was put aboard, the eight passengers waved farewell, and Captain James Watkinson lifted his voice in command. Sailors scurried aloft to cast off the gaskets, topsails were sheeted home, lines were hauled in, and the packet ship *James Monroe,* amid the astonished cheers of the spectators, slid down the river. "Rich cargoes once a month," crowed the New York *Gazette,* "breasting the surge at all seasons of the year." The first regularly scheduled transatlantic liner had sailed.

There was little difficulty in filling the holds of the packets bound for a growing America. Indeed, new lines soon sprang up, to London and Le Havre as well as to Liverpool. The Liverpool packets freighted the most valuable cargoes: English cutlery, hardware, and fine cotton and woolen goods. Le Havre packets carried vintage wines, rich silks, colorful ribbons and laces, and the latest news from the French fashion world. From London came a jumble of wares: books, chronometers, spices, twine, seeds.

But the problem was to find cargoes for Europe that were equally profitable. In the South, Yankee ship owners found what they were looking for: raw cotton for the hungry looms of England and France. The cotton growers were used to shipping their crop directly to Europe, but a few enterprising New Yorkers had a better idea - why not bring the cotton to New York and load it into their packets?

It took a bit of doing. From the North came men to lend money to the cotton farmers, and others to organize a cotton market, and still others to ship the cotton north in coastal packets. Before long, the shrewd Yankees had much of Dixie's cotton in their fists and, for years to come, cargoes for the holds of their ships.

But even with cargoes assured for both western and eastern passages, the ship owners still had problems. On the one hand, they needed fast ships that could outstrip all rivals. On the other, they wanted ships with plenty of cargo space, since this was how they made money.

A knife blade will cut through water faster than a cigar box; just so, a long, narrow ship, with a V-shaped bottom and a sharp bow to cleave through the waves, will out-sail a fat tub of a ship with a bluff bow that butts against the waves. On the other hand, a cigar box carries more than a knife blade. The sharpest ships could carry so little cargo that ship owners called them "pickpockets."

And so a compromise was worked out: bluff-bowed ships with deep, V-shaped bottoms, heavily sparred so that they could carry a great press of sail and sturdy enough to survive the punishment of the westward passage in winter weather. They were entrusted to captains who drove them day and night, fair weather or foul, under as much canvas as they could carry without being wrenched apart.

A captain of an ocean packet stood at the peak of his profession. He had to be an expert seaman and navigator. And he had to have, as well, iron strength and endurance. He alone was responsible for the safety of his ship. He alone had to decide how hard she could be driven and how much punishment she could take from the icy gales and mountainous waves that swept the North Atlantic. In the worst weather, he was always on deck, his ear cocked for the sound of peril in creaking hull or straining spars, always alert for the split-second decision that might mean safety or disaster. He might not go below for days, taking what rest he could in an armchair lashed to the rail. It was not a life for any ordinary person.

Such a captain drove both his ship and his crew of two or three dozen. It took an extraordinary master to get obedience when he ordered his crew aloft during a lull in a gale to shake a reef out of a frozen sail. They might have to climb 100 feet up ice-coated rigging and, swaying back and forth while the wind clawed at them, untie frozen knots with frozen fingers, knowing all the while that as soon as they were safely down, they might be ordered aloft yet again to reef that very same sail. Sailors can get killed obeying orders like that - and many were. Still, the packet captains were obeyed, and by some of the roughest and toughest ever to sail before the mast.

The crews of the early packets were mostly American youngsters, eager to obey because they considered the job only a steppingstone to a command. But the wages - about $15 a month - scarcely paid for the dangers. So when the American merchant marine pushed its way into new trade routes, these youngsters gradually left the packets to learn their ropes on easier voyages.

Their places were taken either by greenhorns who knew no better or by ruffians from the squalid waterfronts of Liverpool and New York, the sailors called "packet rats." To prove how tough they were, they would go anywhere and do anything. They had no morals; they would rob a passenger or knife an officer. To force obedience, officers often had to feed the crew "handspike hash" or "belaying-pin soup."

Perhaps, just after a packet captain had dealt with a mutinous seaman, he would find himself entertaining at his dinner table royalty, diplomats, or international celebrities such as Nathaniel Hawthorne or Charles Dickens. This, too, was his job, and he did it well.

Stern disciplinarian, superb navigator, gracious host - all these a captain had to be, and his fame grew with the ships he commanded. So did his income. His salary was ridiculous - never much more than $30 a month - but there were "perquisites." He could, if he chose, bring his wife and family along free. He also got a percentage of passenger fares, freight charges, and mail postage, enough to bring him as much as $20,000 a year - a princely income for those days.

He was worth it. In his hands, the packet ships slashed the time to and from Europe.

The passage east to Europe was called "downhill," thanks to the prevailing winds that blow from west to east. Back to America, the passage was "uphill," for not only did a ship buck the prevailing winds, she also had to battle the Gulf Stream current.

Tacking all the way, she might log as much as 1,000 miles more sailing uphill than down. Before the packets, the downhill passage took a month or more, while three months was not unusual for climbing uphill.

But the early packets of the Black Ball Line averaged less than twenty-five days to Europe and only forty-three days back again. Indeed, in 1823, a little Black Ball packet, the *New York,* raced downhill to Liverpool in fifteen days, sixteen hours, a record that was to stand for fourteen years.

But sailing with or into the wind, the packets raced. America was in a hurry, building, growing, and expanding. Still not self-sufficient, the nation needed manufactured goods, textiles, iron, and steel from England and Europe. The packets were the main conveyer belt for this stream of goods.

The belt moved faster and ever faster. Then, as now, speed was the passion of the day. The packets were the queens of the Atlantic: They won the passengers and the mails and the most valuable freight. And their captains, as exclusive as they were famous, were the kings.

It was into this select fraternity that Nat Palmer stepped when he took command of the *Huntsville,* a coastal packet carrying cotton from New Orleans to New York. Safe and fast runs were as important in this trade as they were on the North Atlantic run.

For the competent master of a coaster, it was but a step to the quarterdeck of a transatlantic packet.

The *Huntsville's* owner was a remarkable little man named Edward Knight Collins, who liked to wear a high hat so that he would look taller. Three years younger than Palmer, and like him, a Yankee, Collins had had the same sort of adventurous youth, learning about pirates and shipwrecks in the West Indies trade while he was still in his teens. At thirty, he was operating the Louisiana & New York Line, a fleet of five coastal packets. These ships were bigger and better than those of his competitors; by hiring captains like Nat Palmer, Collins meant to make sure that his ships were also faster.

The passage from New Orleans to New York took, on the average, eighteen days. Palmer, in the *Huntsville,* cut the time to fourteen.

Collins was delighted, as much by the shorter time as by Palmer's gracious ways with the rich southern planters who were his passengers. For his part, Palmer was delighted with the *Huntsville,* for she had taught him a brand-new lesson - a ship with flat floors, that is, with a U-shaped bottom, could also be a fast ship. (A debate had gone on for centuries as to whether a flat-floored craft could out-sail a craft with a V-shaped bottom. Palmer proved conclusively that it could.)

All five Collins packets were relatively flat-floored, but the reason had nothing to do with speed. Mud flats and sand bars filled the mouth of the Mississippi. The early coastal packets with their deep V-shaped bottoms got stuck on these flats; the Collins packets were built with flat floors to permit them to sail in the shoal water to the New Orleans docks beyond.

But to say these ships were fast because they were flat-floored seemed outlandish to most shipbuilders. They had always held that a deep V-shaped bottom was needed for speed. Palmer did not think so. And Collins listened to what Palmer had to say.

Collins was a shrewd man, and ambitious; he dreamed of launching his own line of transatlantic packets. He was also the kind of man who liked new ideas. Perhaps Palmer's theory of design pointed the way toward the perfect compromise - a swift ship that would still carry a big cargo.

Collins sent Palmer to Liverpool to see if there might be room for still another transatlantic packet service. Meanwhile, the chances are he studied the latest packets to see what his competitors were building. If he did, he noticed that the bow, which had been so bluff, was growing sharper. And sure enough, the deep, V-shaped bottom was less pronounced than it had been a few years before.

In any event, when Nat Palmer came back from Liverpool and reported that the British would welcome a new line, Collins made his decision. He would build the biggest and most luxurious packet ships in the world. They would be designed by Palmer, and they would be, as Palmer had suggested, flat-floored.

These were the ships of the Dramatic Line, each named for a theatrical celebrity: the *Shakespeare,* the *Garrick,* the *Sheridan,* the *Siddons,* and the *Roscius.* Their new design set tongues wagging all up and down the New York waterfront and especially at the East River shipyard of Brown & Bell where Collins's new ships were built. Even the builders were skeptical. "They'll never make the passage to the west'ard," they insisted. But Palmer, who supervised their construction, was unmoved.

Nor was he wrong. In 1839, on the westward run, the Dramatic packets clipped twelve days off the forty-three-day average of the early Black Ballers. Moreover, a U.S. Navy commodore admitted that the *Siddons* or the *Roscius* could out-sail any American warship of the day. And yet, they freighted more cargo than their competitors. The Dramatic packets were "the pride of New York and the marvel of Liverpool." Other shipbuilders raised their eyebrows and thoughtfully fingered their beards. Soon the influence of these Collins-Palmer packets would be seen, not only in the transatlantic packets, but also in the ships being built for the growing China trade.

Captain Nat personally commanded the first three Dramatic packets to be launched. On these runs he strengthened his reputation as a driver who was ready to push his ship to the very brink of disaster and then hold her there. But, by the time he was in his forties, even so daring and rugged a captain as Palmer hankered for an easier way of life than the transatlantic packet race. Just as his ideas about ship design had found their way into the new Canton packets, so Captain Nat found himself lured by the China run. He could make quite as much money, he thought, and his life would be far more serene.

In January 1843, Nat Palmer stood on the quarterdeck of the *Paul Jones,* bound east for China. He stood, as well, on the threshold of the clipper-ship era, the time of his country's greatest glory on the seas.

2
THE LURE OF THE ORIENT

The China trade had long beckoned to the more adventurous of America's mariners with the promise of excitement and the possibility of profits. The excitement was free. It ranged from fierce typhoons and bloodthirsty pirates to the wonders wild and new of a strange country that had long remained forbidden to foreigners. The profits, while not so certain, could be astronomical.

The first European vessel ever seen in a Chinese port arrived at Canton in 1516. She was Portuguese and her sailors, with noses like great beaks, both frightened and amused the Chinese. They did not know whether these outlandish foreigners were men or devils. The Portuguese traded their cargo of spices for silks and camphor and then sailed peacefully away. Later, more Portuguese came, but these killed and robbed, and the Chinese had their answer. Foreigners were devils.

The rulers of China were proud and civilized. They believed their vast country, the Flowery Land, to be "all that was under heaven," and their emperor to be the representative of God on earth. Their vision of life was that all men should live harmoniously with each other and with God and nature. After they saw what the Portuguese had done, they tried to keep all foreign "barbarians" at arm's length.

But the riches of China were a golden lure. Over the years, the Portuguese were so persistent that at last the Chinese reluctantly permitted trade with the "foreign devils." They allowed the Portuguese to live in a tiny colony called Macao, limited their trade to Canton, and surrounded them with rules and regulations. In 1634 came the Dutch, the "Ho-lan devils," and a few years later, the English, the "red-haired devils." (When the Americans arrived after the Revolution, the Chinese called *them* the "flowery-flag devils.")

A small group of Chinese merchants - the Co-Hong - was made responsible for all trade. The foreign "factories," or Hongs, in which the Europeans had their offices, their living quarters, and their warehouses, were in a special area outside the walls of Canton. Also in this area were the Hongs of the

Chinese merchants. No women were allowed at the Hongs nor guns or arms of any kind. Foreigners could not enter the city of Canton; their ships had to anchor at Whampoa, a dozen miles downstream. And when the shipping season was over in March, the foreigners had to return to Macao.

One further precaution was taken by the Chinese. It was forbidden to teach their language to foreigners. The result was a business language called Pidgin English (Pidgin was a corruption of the word "business") made up of English, Chinese, Indian, and Portuguese words. Conversation in Pidgin, with a Chinese accent and decorated with Chinese images, sounded like singsong baby talk. A brig, for instance, was called a "two-piecey bamboo," a full-rigged ship a "three-piecey bamboo."

Europeans resented these rules, but to disobey them meant that all trade would be stopped. As a matter of fact, this unique trade had its advantages. The Hong merchants were intelligent, well-bred, and completely honorable in their dealings. Furthermore, they did everything in their power to make the life of the foreigners at Canton as smooth and pleasant as possible. Houqua, for a number of years the head of the Co-Hong, was especially beloved by the Americans.

But permitting foreigners to buy their teas and silks and other goods was as far as the Chinese would go. "The Celestial Empire possesses all things in prolific abundance," the emperor proclaimed. "There is therefore no need to import the manufactures of outside barbarians. . . ." This meant that Chinese goods had to be paid for in specie - gold or silver coin - unless something could be found that the Chinese would buy.

As it happened, the Americans had one thing they knew the Chinese would buy - ginseng root. The Chinese believed that eating it would make them immortal. Ginseng grew, conveniently, in the forests of New York and New England. Right after the Revolution, when for the first time an American vessel, the *Empress of China,* sailed for Canton, she carried thirty tons of ginseng root and some fur skins.

When they learned that the profits from this one voyage were over $30,000, other daring young Americans promptly set their sails for Canton - and adventure.

Adventure there was aplenty. Ginseng would not pay for all the goods the Americans wanted. And so they scurried all over the world to find other articles to tempt the Chinese.

Otter skins were prized by wealthy Chinese officials, known as mandarins, who used them to trim their robes. This led Yankee captains to range the northwest coast of America and trade with hostile Indians for the skins. Others searched the tropical islands of the Pacific for sandalwood, and for bêches-de-mer (sea cucumbers), sharks' fins, and edible birds' nests to tickle the Chinese palate. Still others, like Nat Palmer, scoured the Antarctic and the South Seas for sealskins. And by the time the otters and the seals were nearly exterminated, America had begun to manufacture cotton goods that the Chinese would buy. Yet, for many years, Americans still had to freight kegs of specie to pay for the Chinese teas and silks.

The British, with their constant demand for tea (which led the Chinese to believe, perhaps correctly, that they could not live without it), resorted more and more to a cargo which, although forbidden in China, they knew they could sell. This was opium. They grew the dangerous drug in India, shipped it in swift opium clippers, and smuggled it into China.

One of the first British opium clippers was the *Red Rover,* a copy of a famous American privateer, the *Prince de Neufchâtel.* The word clipper means that which moves or flies swiftly, and at this time, it meant any small, fast vessel designed for speed. Baltimore was famous for such swift craft. Long, low, and flush-decked, the Baltimore clippers had won their reputation as pirate craft, as illegal slavers, or as privateers during the War of 1812.

The opium clippers faced the same perils that all shipping faced in the China seas. First were the seas them-selves, filled with uncharted sand bars and reefs, snarling with swift and changeable currents. Then there were the monsoons. From October to April, they blew out of the northeast; from April to October, they came violently from the southwest, bringing rain. Most mariners timed their voyages so as to be blown up to China by the southwest monsoon, and down again by the northeast monsoon - one round trip a year.

But not the opium clippers. They were expected to make two or even three voyages between India and China each year and therefore had been designed with tall raking masts, slender hulls, and the most effective rigs for beating to windward. Double crews handled the great press of canvas that they spread to the winds. The *Red Rover*'s first voyage to China against the monsoon was hailed as "astonishing" and "unparalleled," for until then, not even the finest British warship had been able to accomplish such a feat.

While the foulest weather in these waters was the typhoon - its shifting winds could in an instant set a ship aback and drive her under by the stern, or snap her masts - the most fearful danger was piracy. The pirates preyed on all shipping, but the opium clippers and their valuable cargoes were their favorite game. Along nearly every channel of the Malay Archipelago, pirates lay in wait, cunning, cruel men who thought nothing of slicing off a head, or if they took prisoners, either holding them for ransom or enslaving them.

When a ship was so unlucky as to run on a reef or be idled by a calm, her crew loaded their cannons and oiled their muskets; in the galley, even the cook made ready his own weapons - large kettles of boiling water with which to scald any marauder. Before long, the Malay pirates would appear, circling about in long, swift proas. Then, yelling and brandishing their razor-sharp krisses, they would try to storm aboard.

Chinese pirates infested the islands that freckled the Canton estuary, and their attacks were as noisy as they were deadly. They clashed gongs, beat drums, and shrieked and howled as they fired their muskets and tossed their firebrands.

The mandarins, when they captured a pirate, did their best to make his punishment fit his crime. They subjected Apootsae, a celebrated cutthroat, to a terrible finish. He was slowly and deliberately sliced into small pieces, a punishment called the Thousand Cuts.

The best insurance against piracy was speed, and speed was expensive. The *Red Rover* carried a crew of 150 men, well-paid not only to sail but also to fight. Yet the owners of the opium clippers could shrug off such expenses. They were a drop in the ocean compared to their profits.

The Americans also dealt in opium. They imported it from Turkey - their only source of supply - and they also acted as agents in selling the Indian crop of the drug. The most active of the American firms in this trade was Russell & Company. In small American-built clipper schooners, they ran opium from the island of Lintin to various stations on the China coast, whence it was smuggled into the interior.

Why this ugly traffic in narcotics? One member of Russell & Company had an answer: The profits were fat and easy. All that was required was to ignore the small voice of conscience. Only one American firm heeded that voice. This was Olyphant & Company, nicknamed "Zion's Corner."

The Chinese called opium "foreign mud" and bitterly resented the vicious traffic. At length, in 1839, the Chinese emperor determined to stop it.

He sent to Canton a special envoy, a black-bearded man named Lin, who, by threatening the death penalty, forced the English to turn over 20,000 chests of opium worth $12 million. The British government was outraged at this move by the Chinese. It demanded an apology, payment for the opium, relaxation of trade restrictions, and the opening of other ports to trade. The British used Lin's seizure of the drug as their excuse for waging a war on the defenseless Chinese people, who suffered enormous losses in both lives and property.

This dishonorable aggression, known as the Opium War, came to an end in 1842 with the signing of the Treaty of Nanking. It gave the English everything they wanted, including the island of Hong Kong, from which they continued to smuggle opium into China in even greater quantities. In 1844, the United States, taking advantage of this opening of China, negotiated a treaty that also gave its ships access to additional ports.

These events in China set the stage for the coming of the clipper ships. In America, in the meantime, other forces had been at work.

The prospect of profits made for faster ships. The opium clippers would never have been built if their cargoes had not made fabulous profits for their owners. So with the China clippers; if speed had not paid off, they would never have come to be.

The sailing track from New York to Canton stretched over 16,000 sea miles. Back in 1784, it took the *Empress of China* almost six months to sail to China and, after waiting for her cargo and the favorable monsoon, four-and-a-half months to come back - in all, about a year and four months. For the next thirty years, the average time for a voyage out and back remained the same, a year or more. But by the 1830s, runs of 100 days in either direction had become common, and always waiting to sail with the favorable monsoon, the time out and back to China was cut to an average of nine months.

These faster voyages were not due to changes in ship design, but to the same technique that made for the speedy packet runs - hard, incessant driving. Indeed, a number of those same old packets were transferred to the China run, and in 1837, one of them, the *Silas Richards,* sped home from Canton in ninety-four days.

The China merchants pricked up their ears. Faster voyages meant more voyages in a year and therefore more money in the bank. Then, too, speed was important because of the nature of the cargo which, by 1840, was largely tea.

Tea is delicate and spoils quickly. Not only did fast runs mean less spoilage, but the merchant whose ship was first home with the new crop could expect a profit of as much as 150 percent; the man whose tea arrived in a slow boat from China might find the market glutted.

Although tempted by the coin-clinking advantages of speed, until 1839 no China merchant would risk building a fast ship. "It don't pay to go fast and carry nothing" was still their attitude. Moreover, they had before them the example of the *Ann McKim.*

The *Ann McKim* had been built in Baltimore in 1833. Her lines were those of a Baltimore clipper schooner, enlarged and rigged as a ship. While she lived up to the reputation of all Baltimore clippers for grace and speed, she could carry very little cargo.

Not until Collins's Dramatic Line packets proved that the same flat floors that gave a ship more cargo space also gave her greater speed did a few merchants begin to think about building faster ships for the China trade. Nat Palmer's *Paul Jones* and two or three other fast Canton packets were laid down, and they proved successful on the China run, but there was no clamor for more. It took the Opium War and the opening of new ports to provide the final stimulus for building the majestic China clippers.

The credit for developing the China clippers rests with two New York houses, A. A. Low & Bros, and Howland & Aspinwall. Abbott Low and his brothers were the sons of a Salem drug merchant, who imported from the Orient wonderfully exotic wares - mocha, gum arabic, asafetida, and musk in pods. Seth Low had a dozen children. There were always so many Lows underfoot in Salem that someone made up a jingle about them:

"Old Low, old Low's son,

Never saw so many Lows since the world begun."

One after another, Abbott Low and his brothers sailed for Canton to work for Russell & Company. By 1841, Abbott, having made his fortune at Canton, was back in New York doing business as a merchant in the China trade.

As it happened, Abbott's brother William was at Macao when the *Paul Jones* and Nat Palmer arrived in 1843. He and his wife sailed back with Captain Nat. For both the Lows and Palmer, it was a momentous voyage.

On the way out to China, Captain Nat's lively mind had been judging the performance of the *Paul Jones,* figuring out how her design could be improved for this belt of weather, how altered for that. But not until the homeward run did he face his first monsoon. It was tack and tack again as the *Paul Jones* slowly clawed her way down the turbulent China seas.

An old driver like Nat Palmer was not one to accept with resignation whatever weather nature put in his way. No wind at all enraged him. "He would come on deck with an old white beaver hat on," a mate recalled, "take it off, and stamp on it, and damn the calm and everything else." As for losing time by having to beat against a monsoon, that set his temper boiling even hotter. His mind bubbled with ideas for a design that would lick this black beast of a China run.

After the China seas were passed, Captain Nat's temper cooled to the point where he could talk to William Low about his ideas for a sharp ship that would thumb its nose at the monsoons. Palmer whittled away at a model, and before the *Paul Jones* reached New York, the two men had agreed to build their ship.

Abbott Low enthusiastically endorsed the idea. Palmer was to have a quarter interest; the Lows would take care of the rest. Contracts for the building of the ship were let at once. She was to be called the *Houqua,* in honor of the Canton merchant so beloved by the Americans who dealt with him.

The *Houqua* was launched in the spring of 1844. "We never saw a vessel so perfect in her parts," the New York *Herald* reported. "As sharp as a cutter - as symmetrical as a yacht - as rakish in her rig as a pirate - and as neat in her deck and cabin arrangements as a lady's boudoir. . . . Her bows are as sharp as a pair of Chinese shoes." But not even the *Herald*'s reporter was aware that, as the *Houqua* slid down the ways, the era of the American clipper ship had been born.

With Captain Nat on the quarterdeck watching her performance as closely as a mother-bear her cub, the *Houqua* sailed for Canton on the last day of May 1844.

While the *Houqua* was being built, in a nearby yard, another ship was growing in the stocks. Commissioned by Howland & Aspinwall and designed by a young man named John Griffiths, she was called the *Rainbow.*

John Griffiths was a new breed of cat in the world of ship design, the first naval architect.

Before him, in the world's long history of ships under sail, vessels had been planned by men whose ideas for mold and rigging came from their experience as mariners (like Nat Palmer), or from their hit-or-miss experience as shipbuilders. In short, knowledge of ship design was based on trial and error. Griffiths applied science and mathematics.

While working as a Navy draftsman, he wrote articles on naval architecture and read everything he could find on the subject. One book led him to test the resistance offered by different shapes when pulled through a tank of water. His experiments led him to some unusual conclusions as to the most efficient design for a fast ship.

In 1841, while employed as a draftsman for a New York shipbuilder, Griffiths lectured on his ideas at the American Institute. He was ignored. The next year his lecture, illustrated with a model he had built, met with the same reception that has been accorded all unfamiliar ideas down through the centuries. His audience handed him a horselaugh.

Nevertheless, Howland & Aspinwall were daring enough to gamble on Griffiths' untried design. It was not an easy decision, for it meant risking $45,000, but the odds were inviting. If Griffiths was right, the partners knew they would recoup their investment in no time at all.

Howland & Aspinwall had bought the *Ann McKim* and put her on the China run; they had bought one of Collins's old flat-floored "cotton wagons," the *Natchez,* and sent her to the Orient as well. And when each of these came home in less than 100 days, the temptation was overwhelming to see what a brand-new sharp ship, designed especially for the China run, could do. And so Howland & Aspinwall commissioned the *Rainbow.*

But before long, the partners began to worry excessively. Men along the waterfront hooted at the *Rainbow* as she grew in the stocks. Her bows were turned inside out, said the experts; she was so sharp that come the first big wave, she would knife under and never be seen again. Some said if she were turned around and the rudder attached to her bow, she might sail very well, indeed.

Howland & Aspinwall ordered all work stopped and wrangled with Griffiths: It was not too late, he could still heed the experts and change the *Rainbow*'s design. But Griffiths refused. And so, finally, the partners sighed and agreed to let him proceed. The delay, however, meant that the *Rainbow,* whose keel had been laid some months before that of the *Houqua,* was not launched until early in 1845, long after Nat Palmer had sailed for China.

"The *Rainbow,* a new clipper for the China trade . . . holds out a promise of great speed," the New York *Herald* proclaimed at her launch. Her owners must have offered a hopeful "Amen," crossed their fingers, and then sat back to wait and see.

There is an old and endless argument as to which was the first of the clipper ships. Some point to the *Ann McKim,* some to the *Houqua,* and some say the *Rainbow* was the first.

But what was a clipper? It was a ship (technically a three-masted, square-rigged sailing vessel) built to carry cargo rather than passengers. And what made a clipper ship different from all other sailing ships? According to Carl Cutler, an authority on the subject, there were two differences. For a ship to qualify as a clipper, she had to be sharp - that is, her hull designed "for speed rather than cargo space." And second, she had to be "extremely heavily sparred, in order to spread a far larger area of canvas than ships of equal size were accustomed to spread." And then he added a third factor, without which "the finest ship that ever floated was a beautiful fabric and nothing more" - she had to have as her master a driver, a "daredevil with a mania for speed."

The truth is that there was no first clipper ship. America had long known how to build and sail fast vessels, and sharp ships had been built before the *Ann McKim.* Most pilot boats in New York harbor had the same long, sharp, hollow bows that the experts had proclaimed would prove the end of the *Rainbow.* What was revolutionary was that known principles of design were refined and combined in unusual ways.

But if there is no "first" clipper, there is no doubt about one thing. Nat Palmer on the *Houqua* and Captain John Land on the *Rainbow* were daredevils who could be counted on to test a ship's speed to the edge of disaster.

The *Houqua* sped swiftly along on her first voyage - ninety-five days out and ninety days home. Captain Nat was pleased. The *Rainbow* did not do so well. Only a few days out of New York, Captain Land piled on so much sail that she lost her topgallant masts and very nearly did drive herself under for good. But this was part of learning the temperamental ways of a ship. Coming home, still learning, Captain Land drove all the rest of the sails out of her. It was a disappointing voyage - 108 days out and 102 days home.

But Howland & Aspinwall were not concerned about the *Rainbow*'s record. She was scarcely out of New York harbor when something happened that pushed her completely out of their minds. Captain Robert Waterman brought their old cotton tub, the *Natchez,* home from Macao in seventy-eight days. New York was electrified. How had Waterman accomplished such a miracle? The rumor went around that he had found a new and shorter route home from the East.

The truth was much simpler. Waterman, a handsome, powerful man, was one of the hardest drivers in the business. He had gone to sea when he was twelve, and by the time he was twenty-four, he was one of the elite - the master of a Black Baller. He had turned from the Atlantic packets to the South American trade; when the *Natchez* was diverted to the China run, it was Waterman's hand that held the whip. That hand spared neither his ship, his crew, nor himself.

When a ship left port under Waterman it might look like an ordinary sailer; but when she came tearing home she would have sprouted new wings, would have flung new canvas to the winds where none had ever been seen before, and groaning and creaking in protest, would have carried that canvas in fair weather and foul long after any other master would have given orders to reef or furl.

Carrying sail in this way was frightening. Waterman had to resort to the iron discipline of the belaying pin and handspike to get his orders obeyed. It was said he even put padlocks on the halyards to keep terrified sailors from taking matters into their own hands and letting sails go on the run. When he reached home port, he could count on loud squawks from some members of the crew because of his hard-driving methods. This time, however, Waterman was hailed as a conquering hero, given an ovation, and pursued by crowds of people eager to wring his hand.

Howland & Aspinwall delighted in all this free and profitable publicity. If Waterman could bring the *Natchez* home in such a short time, what might he do with a ship built for speed? They asked John Griffiths to design a still larger and faster ship especially for Waterman and the China run.

She was to be called the *Sea Witch,* and even before her launch, much was expected of her. For the *Rainbow,* on her second China run, had just romped home in seventy-nine days.

As with the *Rainbow,* the peculiar model and sharp bows of the *Sea Witch* caused comment while she was still being built. Nat Palmer looked her over and reported that she was "likely to prove very swift afloat," but, "being very heavily sparred, will sail at great expense, to say nothing of the wear and tear."

Heavily sparred she was, indeed. Griffiths had consulted with Waterman on her sail plan, with the result that the *Sea Witch* was the tallest ship afloat, spreading more canvas than a seventy-four-gun man-of-war three times her size. In December 1846, sparred and rigged high and low to catch vagrant breezes and hold following winds, and with the house flag of Howland & Aspinwall flying at her main-truck, the *Sea Witch* sailed for Canton. It was the beginning of an illustrious career that would lead her to immortality in the annals of sailing ships.

The Lows, however, were not content to let Howland & Aspinwall capture all the glory and all the profits. In spite of the fact that there were some forty ships plying their way between China and New York, their little *Houqua* had been making money for them and shaving records. They felt another faster and larger ship would surely pay.

Again Nat Palmer did the honors as designer. The new ship was to be slightly larger than the *Sea Witch*. She was called the *Samuel Russell* in honor of the founder of the China trading firm, and in the back of everyone's mind was the thought that she would rival the *Sea Witch*. But even before the launch of the *Samuel Russell,* the *Sea Witch* threw down the gauntlet. Waterman brought her home from China in eighty-one days, a record for sailing against the monsoon, the first record in her fabulous career.

For Waterman, there was to be no rest. Shortly after he landed in New York, he was pursued by policemen seeking to serve him with papers sworn to by members of his crew who were trying to sue him for damages.

Waterman managed to evade the law until the day he was to sail again. Then, while in the offices of Howland & Aspinwall, across the cobblestone street from the dock where the *Sea Witch* lay, he learned that the only exit was blocked by a policeman. Waterman grinned. He had a block and tackle rigged from the roof of the building to the foremast of the *Sea Witch*, called for a bosun's chair, and soon was soaring high above the clutches of the law. Then he really showed his heels. For in an incredible sixty-three minutes, the *Sea Witch* raced the nineteen miles down the bay to the open sea.

When the *Samuel Russell* sailed a few weeks later, she was given a rousing send-off, typical of the interest Americans of that time took in ships and shipping. "Look at the crowds of water-gazers there," Herman Melville wrote of Manhattan. "Posted like silent sentinels all around the town, stand thousands upon thousands of mortal men fixed in ocean reveries. Some leaning against the piles; some seated upon the pierheads; some looking over the bulwarks of ships from China; some high aloft in the rigging, as if striving to get a still better seaward peep. . . ."

At what? The magic of faraway lands? China was closer now - only seventy-eight days away. Who knew how much closer it might be tomorrow? Bigger and faster packets were being built, bigger and faster steamships, bigger and faster clippers. Each new speed record was reported with excitement by the newspapers. Launchings were covered the way drama critics today cover the opening of a play. "Strikingly beautiful," one paper had said of the *Samuel Russell*, "with a dashy, man-of-war air."

The *Sea Witch's* spell was strong. She set the pace for the China fleet on the westward runs; on her next passage home, she shaved the record again. And then in March 1849, as she raced toward port, the watchers at the telegraph station in New York's lower bay could hardly believe their eyes - no China ship was due for at least two weeks. But there she was. Waterman had brought her home in a magical seventy-four days, fourteen hours, to set the world's first permanent sailing record. No later, larger, or sharper clipper ever touched this mark.

She was a lovely ship, the *Sea Witch,* with a lovely name, and her magic was always with her. She broke or set more records than any sailing ship of her size has ever done, before or since.

If the *Samuel Russell* could not lower the time of the *Sea Witch* on the run from Canton to New York, at least she could whip her in the other direction. Although she carried one-fifth less canvas, many considered her not only the equal of the *Sea Witch* but the finest ship afloat. One tea merchant had such confidence in her that he let others pay the highest prices for the first tea on the market; he waited three weeks to buy until prices were lower, knowing that the *Samuel Russell* would still get his tea to New York first.

There was glory aplenty for both the *Sea Witch* and the *Samuel Russell.*

Howland & Aspinwall built no more clippers for China. (Early in 1848, their *Rainbow* sailed out of New York for Valparaiso and was never seen again.) The Lows, however, added still another Palmer-designed clipper to the fleet. This was the *Oriental,* and she was to create a sensation in England after the repeal of the British Navigation Laws in 1849.

These laws had provided that all goods bound for England be carried in either British ships or in ships owned by the country of origin of the goods. This meant that Americans could not compete for the rich trade between England and the Orient. Without such competition, British ship owners felt no need to improve their vessels. This stuffy attitude affected the way the British sailed their ships as well. On the ships of the British East India Company, for example, the custom for years had been to take in all light sail every evening no matter how fine the weather, and this habit persisted. Where American sailors had been trained as daredevils, British sailors had been trained to caution.

The *Oriental* on her second run from America to China established a record that still stands. She made Hong Kong in eighty days, ten hours, the fastest eastward run from either the United States or from England. Russell & Company immediately chartered her to carry tea to England.

There were plenty of English ships in China waiting to carry tea to London at £3.10 per ton, but because of her speed, British merchants were willing to pay a premium of £6 a ton to ship in the *Oriental*. She sailed for London with a cargo of 1,600 tons of tea. This meant that the Low brothers received $48,000 in freight money for this one run - almost two-thirds of what it had cost them to build the ship.

Ninety-seven days after she had left China, the *Oriental* was in London's West India docks - in its time, a record passage, and one that has rarely been surpassed. (By comparison, the bark *Jeannette*, which had left China three days before the *Oriental*, reached London forty-seven days after her.)

The British were stunned. No American clipper had ever before been seen in an English port. Crowds of Londoners flocked to the docks to glimpse this wonderful ship. "Her arrival," it was said, "aroused as much apprehension and excitement . . . as was created by the memorable Tea Party held in Boston harbor in 1773." Her captain, Theodore Palmer (Nat's brother), was lionized. Her lines were copied by naval architects for the British Admiralty. And the editor of *The Times* sternly warned British shipbuilders: "We must run a race with our gigantic and unshackled rival. It is a father who runs a race with his son. . . . Let our shipbuilders and employers take warning in time. . . . We want fast vessels for the long voyages which otherwise will fall into American hands."

Too late for such a warning; the son had a huge head start in the race with his father. For already a new clipper route had opened up, offering a golden incentive to build still larger and faster ships.

From this handful of clippers in the China trade, the American clipper fleet was to grow by leaps and bounds. Soon her competition would lie far back in her wake. Soon Columbia would truly be the gem of the ocean, her sailing ships supreme on all the seven seas.

More than anything else, it was the gold strike in California that opened the way.

3
CLIPPERS FOR CALIFORNIA

In January 1847, not long after Americans had seized California from Mexico, a settlement called Yerba Buena was renamed San Francisco after the magnificent bay on which it was situated.

Over the years, an occasional warship or whaler had put into this bay, seeking fresh supplies, as had vessels trafficking in hides and tallow. The sleepy village had a population of about 800. Then, in January 1848, gold was discovered at Sutter's Mill. San Francisco and California were forever transformed.

Not till September did the news reach the east coast, and several more months passed before people believed it. Then "yellow fever" struck like an epidemic. Wealth just for the taking! Everyone who could headed west for El Dorado.

There were three ways a man could get to the gold fields. Most Midwesterners went overland, by wagon across the mountains. The second way was by sea to Panama or Nicaragua, overland to the Pacific, and by sea again to California. The third was by sea around Cape Horn. Most Easterners, seafarers for generations, chose either of the sea routes.

By the end of 1849, 775 vessels had sailed for the Golden Gate, delivering 40,000 people to San Francisco. The area was totally unprepared for the hordes of gold seekers. There were few houses and little food. Everyone was intent on one thing only - finding gold.

With everything but gold in short supply, prices skyrocketed. Flour and pork were $40 a barrel. A loaf of bread cost fifty cents. Cheap boots sold for $40, good boots for $100. But if the prices were fabulous, so were the profits, and shippers on the east coast hurried to cash in on this new bonanza.

The only way to get supplies to California was around Cape Horn, 15,000 sea miles from New York to San Francisco. The trip took, on the average, about 200 days. But speed was important to shippers, for no one knew how long the gold rush would last. Moreover, cargo space was at a premium. Spurred by visions of fabulous profits, merchants were willing to pay higher and higher rates to ship their wares. Big, fast ships were needed. The solution seemed to lie in the China clippers.

In January 1850, the *Samuel Russell* sailed for California. She was weighed down like a sand barge with freight that would add $72,000 to her owners' bank balance, more than the original cost of the ship. She arrived in San Francisco in 109 days, and shippers back east had their answer. Two months later, the *Sea Witch* sped from New York to the Golden Gate in ninety-seven days - the first ship to make the passage in under 100 days.

Clearly, clippers were the answer. And now there was another kind of rush for gold, with merchants and speculators eager to build fleet ships. The big China clippers had all been built in New York shipyards. But their capacity was limited, and would-be ship owners turned to yards in Maine, New Hampshire, and Massachusetts.

In the fall of 1850, Boston idlers had the fun of watching two large ships growing in the stocks. The *Surprise,* ordered by the Lows, was the brainchild of a youngster named Samuel Pook. The *Stag Hound,* built for Boston merchants, was the handiwork of Donald McKay. These two men were to become the best and best-known designers of clipper ships.

Pook, who was only twenty-three years old, seemed a very raw hand to entrust with such a vast responsibility as an ocean clipper. He was, however, already an experienced naval architect. His interest in ship design came naturally, for his father had been a shipbuilder for the Navy. Young Pook already had to his credit an ocean-going iron steamer and a sleek clipper-bark.

Donald McKay had been born forty years before on a farm in Nova Scotia and had learned his trade in the New York yards. At sixteen, he apprenticed himself to Isaac Webb, one of New York's master shipbuilders. In his contract, McKay pledged Webb faithful service and obedience for four-and-one-half years; he further promised he would not marry, nor play at cards or dice, nor haunt saloons and dance houses. In return, Webb agreed to teach him the "art, trade, and mystery of a shipcarpenter" and to pay him $2.50 a week in wages and $40 a year for bed, board, and clothing.

Shortly before his term was to end, McKay asked Webb for his release so that he might get married. Webb gave it willingly.

Albenia Boole, McKay's bride, was the daughter of a shipbuilder. Well-educated, able to draw up plans for a vessel and lay them off on a mold-loft floor, she brought McKay the benefits of her education. By day, McKay worked as a journeyman shipwright. In the evening, his wife taught him the theories of marine architecture.

In 1840, McKay began to build packets in Newburyport, Massachusetts; before long, Enoch Train, a Boston merchant and ship owner, helped him set up his own yard in East Boston. The *Stag Hound* was his first clipper. On a December morning in 1850, she was to go into the water.

A launch was always an exciting affair. Two months earlier, thousands of Bostonians had watched Pook's *Surprise* slide down the ways, fully rigged, her three skysail yards crossed and her colors flying. They had never seen a ship so sharp. Would she capsize when she hit the water? But Pook had designed her surely. She floated like the seabird she was, and the Lows gave her builder a bonus of $2,500 and readied her for the California run under the whip hand of Captain Philip Dumaresq, an old China driver.

Now the *Stag Hound* was ready, sleek and sharp, the largest merchant ship in the world at that time. On the morning of her launch, she was in gala attire, flags and bunting whipping in a bitter wind. Ice floated in the cold gray waters of Boston Bay and snow crunched underfoot. By noon, some 12,000 people had gathered, families and friends of the owners, builders, and workmen, and the curious from all walks of life. Spectators perched everywhere or waited in boats that dotted the water around the ways. In a special pavilion were the wives and children of the workmen.

As at all launches, there were anxieties. Are the ways properly greased? Will the chains hold? Will the ship tumble over? For the *Stag Hound,* with the longest and sharpest ends ever seen on a ship, there was a further question - would she be seaworthy?

Walter Restored Jones, whose business it was to insure ships, was as gloomy as a thundercloud. After a long look at her lines, he asked her captain, Josiah Richardson, if he might not be "somewhat nervous in going on so long a voyage in so sharp a ship so heavily sparred." "No," Richardson replied, "I would not go in the ship at all if I thought for a moment she would be my coffin." Then he busied himself with the problem at hand - whether the ship would move. It was so cold, the tallow had frozen on the ways. The launch might have to be postponed. Then from the forge came workmen lugging cans of boiling whale oil. They poured it on the ways, and McKay gave the signal. The bells of Boston pealing noon were echoed by the sound of hammers knocking away the blocks.

The watchers held their breath as the great ship stirred. "There she goes!" they cried, and the foreman smashed a bottle of rum across her forefoot. "Stag Hound!" he shouted, "Your name's Stag Hound!" She slid gracefully into the water. Cheering reverberated across the bay; a cannon roared; a band played lustily.

As the salutes continued, the *Stag Hound*, riding high and light, was brought up by anchors a short distance from shore. The crowd gave a great sigh of satisfaction, as tangible as its cheers. It had been a great moment.

So, in the yards of a half-dozen Atlantic seaports, with increasing frequency as 1850 became 1851, the excitement rose. It was like the excitement that would be aroused, for speeds far greater, a century later at Cape Canaveral.

Speed was the watchword, speed to California. To lower the time to San Francisco was the aim of every clipper-ship owner. To back up this aim, they paid their captains as much as $3,000 for the outward run and offered an extra $2,000 if they made the passage in less than 100 days.

A captain like Philip Dumaresq needed no such incentives. He had always believed that the only way to sail a ship was to pile on as much canvas as possible and keep it there as long as possible. Dumaresq drove the *Surprise* to San Francisco in ninety-six days, at once breaking the record of the *Sea Witch* and establishing the reputation of young Pook.

Then came the *Stag Hound*, heavily sparred and fit to carry almost 6,000 square yards of canvas. She was so sharp that her owners had to pay extra insurance on her. She proved seaworthy, but six days out she was dismasted in a gale. Nevertheless, and despite the fact she had to put in at Valparaiso for five days, she made San Francisco in 113 days, a respectable run. And when she reached her home port she had cleared $80,000 for her Boston owners.

Mandarin, Sea Serpent, Witch of the Wave, Typhoon, Celestial . . .

In 1850, there were twenty new clippers; in 1851, forty more. And another way of cutting the time to California was beginning to be recognized as important, thanks to Lieutenant Matthew Fontaine Maury of the United States Navy.

Maury was an officer who got into trouble for his outspoken criticism of outworn naval procedure and his insistent demands for reform. For his pains, he had been put on the inactive list, but in 1842, he was appointed superintendent of the Bureau of Charts and Instruments. Here the logs of Navy vessels were stored, piled up like junk and forgotten; here, it was imagined, Maury would be forgotten, too.

Maury had been interested in navigation ever since, as sailing master on a Navy sloop, he had looked in vain for charts of winds and currents that would help him navigate Cape Horn. He soon realized that these old logs, far from being junk, were treasure in which were hidden the secrets of navigating the oceans of the world. He went to work to dig these secrets out.

His first *Charts and Sailing Directions,* issued in 1847, recommended the best routes to Europe and South America for each month of the year. Hungry for more data, he urged the masters of all merchant ships to record daily "all observable facts relating to winds, currents, and other phenomena"; he offered his charts free in exchange for such daily logs. In 1848, he found his first taker. Captain Jackson of the *D. C. Wright* followed Maury's suggested route to Rio de Janeiro. Three other vessels followed suit. All shaved ten days from the average passage.

Maury's charts showed where the equatorial doldrums would be the narrowest and how to navigate them; where to lose the northeast trade winds; where to pick up the southeast trades. His advice was for some time ignored. None of the clippers sailing in 1850 used his *Sailing Directions;* only a few did in 1851. But word of them gradually spread.

Shortly after the *Stag Hound* sailed for California, Donald McKay began work on another clipper for his friend Enoch Train. This was the *Flying Cloud,* and she attracted attention while she was still in the stocks. The owners of the Swallow Tail Line of Liverpool packets admired her so much that they offered Train $90,000 for her. It meant a fine profit, and Train accepted. He would regret it.

Hundreds of people visited the *Cloud* while she was loading in New York. She was a beauty, and at 1,782 tons, the largest merchant ship afloat. But in a nearby shipyard, the 2,006-ton *Challenge* was being constructed, the loftiest ship ever for her size, her "spars up near Orion," as one of her crew boasted. She was built for Robert Waterman to "challenge the world afloat." Her launch attracted one of the largest and most excited waterfront crowds ever seen.

It was not the *Challenge,* however, but the *Flying Cloud,* commanded by Captain Josiah Cressy, that made the challenge to all the world afloat. On her maiden run to California (with Maury's *Charts and Sailing Directions* on hand), the *Flying Cloud* sped to the Golden Gate in eighty-nine days and twenty-one hours. Eighty-nine was thereafter the magic number for every other clipper master. But only one other clipper would ever touch that mark.

As the clippers grew larger and more numerous, their captains faced the increasingly serious problem of getting competent crews. The safety of any sailing vessel depends on the men who man her. This was especially true of the heavily-sparred clippers.

Gold caused the shortage of sailors. Seamen's wages ranged from $8 to $15 a month - a pittance for perilous, backbreaking work. No wonder sailors jumped ship at San Francisco and headed for the gold fields. Soon there were not enough seamen to go around. The scarcity hurt ships bound for Europe the worst; even the packet rats had deserted their Atlantic ratholes for California.

Crews were usually hired by shipping masters who paid out advance wages and made sure the crew was aboard on time. But when sailors became scarce, the shipping masters had to turn to keepers of seamen's boardinghouses. These "land sharks," with the three months' wages advanced to all sailors as their prize, rounded up all sorts of riffraff - jailbirds, thugs, bums - and palmed them off as able-bodied seamen.

Their most harmless device was to put a horn on the ground and bid the bums walk around it; later, when they were asked what experience they had had, they could truthfully answer, "I've been around the Horn." The worst trick was kidnapping, or shanghaiing as it was known in San Francisco - slipping a drug into a man's drink as he stood in a waterfront saloon. He would wake up miles out to sea, sick, broke, and bewildered.

Thus many a clipper captain found himself with only a sprinkling of able seamen in the fo'c'sle. If he had packet rats on board he was lucky; they at least were magnificent at making and taking sail. The others, the landlubbers, were good for nothing.

When Robert Waterman sailed for California in the lofty *Challenge,* of his crew of fifty-six "experienced" seamen there were only six who could steer. Waterman debated whether to turn back for a new crew. But the cost decided him. Owners would have had to pay another crew's wages; shippers would lose money because of the delay. He determined to whip these ruffians into a semblance of sailors. He and his mates stuck revolvers in their belts and looked forward to an eventful voyage. They were not disappointed.

One morning when the ship was off Rio, four members of the crew attacked the first mate with knives and nearly killed him before Waterman was able to club them down with a belaying pin. When the ship reached San Francisco, some of the ruffians told lurid tales of crewmen starved to death and of others murdered, shot off a yardarm in a Cape Horn gale. A newspaper printed the story, and the next morning an ugly mob threatened to lynch Waterman and his mate. Testimony from passengers and crew members later showed the charges to be completely false.

For clipper captains desperate for crews to replace deserters, San Francisco in 1852 was, as usual, a madhouse. Everything else had changed. There were more people, more buildings; there was more work, more gaiety, more money. And once again there was a shortage of goods.

In 1849, an egg had cost $1, a suit of clothes $200, and the joke was that the nearest laundry was in Hawaii. Then had come glut. with eastern merchants shipping everything from food and furniture to pianos and perfume. By 1850, there was so much unsold merchandise that crates of it were used to fill mudholes in the streets or as foundations for houses. Throughout 1851, prices had remained low.

But in 1852, goods were scarce again and prices were high: flour up from $8 to $40 a barrel, rice from $0.05 to $0.50 a pound. Once again, freight rates rose; and once again, there was a demand for more clippers, bigger and faster than ever.

Antelope, Golden City, Golden Eagle, Westward Ho . . .

In 1852, sixty-six clippers were launched, and two of them left a mark on the development of all later ships. One was Samuel Pook's *Defiance;* the other, Donald McKay's *Sovereign of the Seas.*

The *Defiance* was nearly flat-bottomed. On her maiden run from the yard at Rockland, Maine, to New York, she sailed to Fire Island Light at eighteen knots per hour and from Fire Island Light to Sandy Hook at twenty knots. (Since a nautical mile - 6,080 feet - is some 15 percent longer than a land mile, the term knots, rather than miles per hour, is used to express a ship's speed. Twenty knots is slightly more than twenty-three miles per hour.) To report such speeds was like reporting the incredible, the fantastic. It convinced the most skeptical of the value of flat floors for speed.

McKay's *Sovereign of the Seas,* 2,421 tons, with a mainmast that reached up 201 feet, and able to carry 12,000 running yards of canvas, was likewise relatively flat-floored. On her maiden run to San Francisco, McKay's brother Lachlan was her captain, and he drove her hard. "It was fearful to see the topmasts bend," wrote one of the passengers of the way the *Sovereign* beat around the Horn. "We hardly dared look aloft lest we should see the whole fabric blown away." Indeed, she was dismasted in a South Pacific gale. Down came her main and fore topmasts, down came her mizzen topgallant mast, to dangle and pound away at her hull.

A timid captain would have ordered the tangle cut away, but McKay ordered it saved. His mate said it could not be done - but it was. The *Sovereign* was hove to, and in twenty-four hours, everything was on board and she was on her way again, ripping off twelve knots under what little sail she could carry. McKay had the crew begin rerigging at once, and the *Sovereign* made San Francisco in 103 days, a champion voyage considering it was sailed in the most evil season of the year, August to November.

The *Sovereign of the Seas* sailed on to Honolulu and then back east around the Horn with a cargo of whale oil. Her run home electrified the shipping world. With a crew of only thirty-four hands (105 was her normal complement) and despite a sprung fore topmast, she logged nineteen knots for three successive hours, averaged 378 miles a day for four consecutive days, and sailed 421 miles in one twenty-four-hour period - the first time any ship, under sail or steam, had ever surpassed 400 miles. She reached New York from Honolulu in a smashing eighty-two days, having earned $135,000 in nine months. To cap it all off, she then broke the record from New York to Liverpool, making the run in thirteen days, thirteen-and-a-half hours.

It was a period when records were threatened on every voyage. In 1852, 115 sharp ships sailed for California, racing against each other and the time of the *Flying Cloud.*

In the fall of that year, Donald McKay's *Flying Fish,* commanded by Edward Nickels, cleared port two days after the *John Gilpin.* She passed the *Gilpin* on the way to the equator, but there in the doldrums, with Cape St. Roque rearing its ugly head, Captain Nickels found himself too far west. For three days, he ignored Maury's *Sailing Directions* and tried to fan east without success. Belatedly heeding Maury, he struck boldly south, crossed the equator, and beat east with ease. But the *Gilpin* had passed him. Off the Horn, the *Fish* came up alongside the *Gilpin,* and Nickels facetiously invited her captain on board for dinner. ("I was reluctantly obliged to decline," Captain Doane of the *Gilpin* noted in his log.) The *Fish* forged ahead, holding her lead past the equator. But the *Gilpin* was gaining. She reached the Farallons, off the Golden Gate, ninety-three days and twenty hours from New York. A day later came the *Flying Fish,* her elapsed time only ninety-two days, four hours.

She had won the race, but Nickels could scarcely rejoice. For he had been becalmed a few miles off the coast for three days; with better luck, he might have lowered the *Flying Cloud*'s record by a full day. And what if he had followed Maury's advice? If he had not wasted those three days back in the Atlantic doldrums, he might have reached the Farallons with a fair breeze and cut three days off the *Cloud's,* mark. It was a bitter reflection.

Indeed, the value of Maury's advice was now recognized on all sides. Soon shipmasters of many countries were keeping logs for him. Saving time meant saving money. It was pointed out that on the outward passages to Rio, California, and Australia alone, Maury was saving shippers the equivalent of $2.25 million a year.

Chariot of Fame, Flying Dragon, Lightfoot, Rapid . . .

In 1853, the demand for clippers reached frenzied heights. People who in the past had never dreamed of owning a ship now wanted a clipper, wanted the fortune they hoped a clipper would bring. Down the ways slid 125 sharp ships. Five were launched in Boston in one day. Were they needed?

Jacob Bell, Flying Childers, Storm, Bald Eagle . . .

They were driven as hard as any had ever been

driven before. Philip Dumaresq brought McKay's *Bald Eagle* to San Francisco in 109 days, boasting that she had never been under close reefs, nor had her courses, spencers, or spanker ever been furled. He himself lost thirty-four pounds.

The *Flying Cloud* and the *Hornet* sailed the closest sailing match in the history of the Horn, leaving New York within a few hours of each other and arriving at San Francisco within forty minutes of each other, 105 days out.

Swordfish, Ringleader, North Wind, Flyaway . . .

They swept through the Golden Gate, unloaded their cargoes, picked up ballast, and headed back around the Horn, or over to China to pick up tea. The cabins of one clipper to China were filled with one hundred coffined Chinese being brought home for burial. The corpses were listed as passengers, charged $75 apiece, and earned the captain his usual allowance for passage money.

They even raced eastward back to Boston around the Horn. Boston's *Northern Light* and New York's *Contest* made a match of it. The *Northern Light* won, setting a mark of seventy-six days, eight hours.

Dashing Wave, Flying Scud, Pride of the Ocean, Young America . . .

William Webb considered the *Young America* his masterpiece. She was an extreme clipper of "matchless symmetry and finish," lofty and heavily sparred. Webb wagered $10,000 that she could beat the *Sovereign of the Seas* in a race from New York to San Francisco. Too late: The *Sovereign* had already been put up for Liverpool; the race was never held.

Morning Light, Neptune's Car, Mischief, Great Republic . . .

With the *Great Republic*, 4,555 tons, Donald McKay finally achieved his goal of building the largest clipper in the world. While loading in New York, she caught fire and burned. But like the phoenix, she rose from the ashes. Captain Nat Palmer bought the wreck and rebuilt it. Reduced to 3,357 tons, and with her sail plan and spars cut down so that she needed only half her original complement of 130 to crew her, she was still the largest merchant ship of her time.

Aurora, Polynesia, Eagle Wing . . .

Although 145 clippers laden with goods sailed for the Golden Gate in 1853, by fall, sailings had become less frequent. Freight rates were dropping.

There were signs in the air, signs that trouble was brewing. Ships were laying over a little longer while awaiting cargoes. Some went immediately into the cotton and lumber trades. Others turned to the detested guano trade, still others to the miserable Asian laborer and slave trades.

Too many ships? Too many people trying to mine the vein? No matter. Freight rates, while lower, were still attractive. And there was still a job to do. Steam could not do it, nor could ships of other countries. Only the fleet and graceful clippers could do the job. And they did it magnificently. It was their year of glory.

4
"A BULLY SHIP AND A BULLY CREW"

On the third of June 1851, the *Flying Cloud* sailed for California on the maiden voyage that was to set such a notable record. Three weeks earlier, another new clipper, the *N. B. Palmer*, had cleared for San Francisco. The newest member of the Low fleet, she was named for their old friend Captain Nat and commanded by young Charles Low. Low took the *Palmer* out in 106 days; ten days later, the *Cloud* arrived, covering herself with glory.

Both ships sailed to China and then on to New York. The *Palmer* bested the *Flying Cloud's* time on both of these runs, but Charles Low itched for another chance to race the *Cloud* around the Horn. He was to get his wish. Both ships were put up for

California. The *Flying Cloud* sailed on May 14, 1852, the *N. B. Palmer* on May 22. Besides her cargo, the *Palmer* carried sixteen passengers, half of them children, and the captain's bride, nineteen-year-old Sally Low. It was her honeymoon voyage.

Suppose the *Palmer* had aboard a passenger with an inquiring mind and a sharp, observant eye. His journal might have read something like this:

May 23. Latitude 40°00'N. Longitude 69° 58'W. Yesterday a magnificent spring day. At Peck Slip where *Palmer* lay, all hurry and bustle. Mates and boys scurried to discharge last-minute duties. Passengers clambered on board, children darting about, excited. Wharf a babble of sound - goodbyes, cheers, tears. Pigs and chickens and the cow penned on deck joined in hubbub.

Tug eased us into East River and down to Battery where we anchored to pick up crew. Thirty-six crew members and baggage brought aboard by boardinghouse runners. (Understand sailor lucky if baggage includes straw mattress - called donkey's breakfast - kitbag or chest containing sou'wester, oilskins, rubber boots, leather belt, knife, blanket, and plug of tobacco.)

Some sailors drunk, some actually unconscious, some gloomy, some cheery. Unconscious hoisted on board, dragged to fo'c'sle to sleep it off. Others mustered aft, and each man questioned as to his experience. Crew doesn't look like much. Hope am wrong.

Captain Low and pilot on quarterdeck. Shipping master and runners ordered ashore. Mate musters crew forward on fo'c'sle head to man capstan bars and heave anchor. This is moment all waiting for - moment for which watchers line Battery shore to hear shanties, songs sailors sing as aid to work. "Come alive men!" mate bawls. "Out of the graveyard!"

Men strain against capstan bars. Tipsy shantyman throws back his head and bursts into song. "A bully ship and a bully crew," he warbles.

"Doo-da," the men chorus, feet shuffling in time. "Doo-da."

"A bully mate and a captain, too."

"Doo-da, Doo-da-day!"

"Then blow ye winds, Hi-oh,

For Cali-for-ny-O.

Oh, there's plenty of gold

So I've been told,

On the banks of the Sac-ra-men-tO."

"Anchor's hove short, sir!" mate calls out. Captain signals tug to pick up slack on towing hawser. Then it's "Heave ahead!" Pawls click. Feet shuffle.

Shantyman sings out, "Round Cape Horn in the month of May."

"Doo-da, Doo-da."

"Round Cape Horn in the month of May."

"Doo-da, Doo-da-day!"

"Then blow ye winds, Hi-oh . . ."

"Anchor's aweigh, sir!" mate shouts. Tug ordered full speed ahead and *Palmer* slowly gets under way. Crowd lining shore raises three cheers to wish clipper well. *Palmer* dips her ensign in reply. We are on our way.

Towed through Narrows and around point of Sandy Hook. Here *Palmer,* till then a lifeless thing of wood, hemp, and canvas, slowly transformed into full-fledged sea bird. White wings spread, strong pinions to carry us swiftly along. Twenty miles out, we drop pilot at pilot boat. Fair wind, all sails set and drawing, we're off.

After crew stowed gear and made all shipshape, Captain Low addressed them from break of quarterdeck. Low a young man (twenty-eight), slight, dark hair, pale, hard blue-gray eyes, looks fit. Told crew they would get good grub and good treatment; they were to answer when spoken to, obey orders quickly and willingly. Said he was a fair-minded captain; they would have a pleasant voyage if they did as ordered. Any insubordination and they would have rough time of it. "I command this ship," he said firmly. "My orders will be obeyed." Believed him. Felt better.

As Captain talked, ship's officers searched crew's dunnage in fo'c'sle, confiscating slingshots, blackjacks, bowie knives, pistols, whiskey. Crew then divided into two watches. Each watch on duty for four hours, then off four. Between 4:00 p.m. and 8:00 p.m. are two two-hour watches - dog watches. These serve to alternate night watches, so same men do not have to stand two-night watches every night.

Second mate's or starboard watch set. Chief mate's or port watch sent below. Still hard to tell what kind of crew we have.

Passengers unpack, get acquainted, inspect home of next three months. *Palmer*'s cabin accommodations very comfortable. Dining room and saloon richly carpeted, separated by paneled and stained glass partitions. Seats plump, comfortable. Eight staterooms, four to a side, paneled in bird's-eye maple and mahogany; wide berths.

Dinner delicious: soup, chickens, vegetables, desserts. Might be on shore. Early to bed, up early for breakfast. Pancakes and bacon. Only lady present Captain's wife. All others seasick. Moderate breeze and pleasant.

May 25. Latitude 37°46' Longitude 61°20'. Past two

days moderate to strong breezes. Last night high head sea.

Life on board ship carefully ordered. Captain responsible for ship and its navigation. Takes observations at noon, sets ship's course, commands her working. Stands no watch, comes and goes as he pleases. Can marry, bury dead, kill in case of mutiny. Absolute ruler. If benevolent, life pleasant. If not, life hell. Captain Low seems benevolent.

Chief mate, Mr. Haines, Captain's right-hand man. Responsible for repair of ship. Sets everyone daily task. Takes own observations. Keeps log. A navigator in own right. Second mate in charge of starboard watch. Leads men in day's work. Third mate assists chief mate.

Crew includes sailmaker, carpenter, cook, steward in charge of cabin, six ordinary and thirty able seamen, and four boys. Mr. Haines reports we are in luck with crew. They seem to be what they claim to be - seamen.

When sailor not actually working ship (making and taking sail, etc.) he works *on* the ship. As Dana says, "A ship is like a lady's watch, always out of repair." Rigging requires constant work - mending, protecting from chafing, replacing. Sails also need mending or replacing. Ordinary seaman needs only know how to furl, reef, and steer. Able seaman also knows how to work on rigging - making knots, splices, seizings - and how to mend a sail. Boys expected to know nothing.

May 26. Latitude 36°32' Longitude 53°10'. Breeze moderating. At noon, Captain Low discovered we made record run of 396 miles in past twenty-four ours. Much pleased. This beat *Flying Cloud's* 374-mile record run by good margin. Also confided his delight at finding his bride to be a good sailor. Mrs. Low has not missed a meal.

Talked to Captain about himself. He said family wanted him to become merchant in family firm, but he hankered for sea. Twice tried to stow away, twice caught. Finally, in 1842, allowed to ship as boy on vessel bound for Canton. After four more China voyages, Low made captain of *Houqua,* age twenty-three. Had sailed in her since her launch. Has twice made Horn passage.

May 29. Latitude 34°01' Longitude 46°00'. Light breeze and pleasant. We speed sweetly along, everything set and straining, our course east by south. Because we depend on winds we cannot sail in straight line for Cape St. Roque, eastern bulge of South America. NE trade winds would push us too far west to round bulge. We must run our easting out in high latitudes using westerly winds to carry us across to NE trades, which will speed us to equator. We log an extra thousand miles but save months. This morning spoke whaler *Atlantic.*

June 1. Latitude 26°06' Longitude 34°16'. Moderate breeze and pleasant. Sailing through variables of Cancer, belt of calms and variable winds called Horse Latitudes. Name originated in colonial days. Vessels from New England bound for West Indies with cargoes of horses often becalmed here. When water supplies dwindled, horses died of thirst and were thrown overboard. Our wind still with us. Crew busy preparing *Palmer*'s oldest and lightest suit of sails for equatorial doldrums. Slatting and slamming of canvas against masts in swells of calms plays havoc with sail.

Day at sea begins early. At 4:30 a.m. (1 bell) cook and steward wakened. At 5:00 (2 bells) coffee served to watch on deck and work begins. From stem to stern decks washed down. All paint wiped with cotton swabs. Meanwhile, Mr. Haines makes his morning inspection. Goes up every mast, onto every yardarm, checks every sail, spar, bolt, band, and rope. Notes repairs and replacements needed. Lives of crew and safety of ship depend on such details. Mate then confers with carpenter, sailmaker, and other officers. They lay out work for day.

Breakfast for crew 7:30, dinner at noon, supper at 5:30. Sailors' mess mainly salt beef and pork (salt junk, they call it), potatoes, beans, hard bread, tea, and coffee. Special treat is plum duff - flour pudding with dried fruit and molasses. Sailors prefer salt junk to fresh meat. Work better on it, know better how to curse it. "When sailors grumble, all is well."

June 3. Latitude 24°03' Longitude 32°39'. Two days of calms. Captain rowed ladies around the *Palmer* so that they might see her with all sails set - even if not drawing. Captain's wife praised her. Mrs. Stout remarked how small she looked, was glad to be back on board.

In the evening, passengers danced on deck by moonlight, sang, and enjoyed the calms. Captain Low impatient.

June 6. Latitude 14°21' Longitude 29°48'. Pleasant trades. Sunday. Ship quiet. Deck scrubbed clean, brass shines. Watch has nothing to do but work ship. Little of that with breeze steady E by S. Crew sits about reading, mending clothes, smoking. Last night, as every Saturday, slop chest opened for crew. From this store they buy what they need - clothing, tobacco, etc. - charging it against wages.

June 8. Latitude 8°44' Longitude 26°54'. Pleasant trades. At 2:00 a.m. came up with and passed to windward of clipper ship *Gazelle,* which sailed five days before us. Captain woke wife and passengers that we might see magnificent sight of clipper under full sail. *Gazelle* beautiful, well-named.

June 12. Latitude 5°49' Longitude 25°14'. Wind let go three days ago, leaving typical equator weather. Calms and cat's paws. Hot damp heat. Everything sticks. Nothing dries. Only motion a slow, deep surge. Sails slap against the masts like pistol shots. Timbers creak. Ship drifts.

Far off a cat's paw ripples the water. Crew quickly braces yards to catch the breeze - their first job in calms, day or night. A sudden squall shatters the mirror sea into angry whitecaps. There is a miniature tempest; the crew is a whirl of activity; then it is gone.

Breath-taking sunsets. Night sky star-spangled. Southern Cross low to the south, soon will be high above us. Night sea ablaze with phosphorus trails. Hot.

Still in company with the *Gazelle*. Some days she gets a breeze, comes up to us. Again, we run away from her.

June 14. Latitude 1°16' Longitude 28°10'. Moderate breezes from S to SSE. *Gazelle* out of sight astern. Captain hopes to cross equator close to Longitude 28°30'W as advised by Maury. We will weather Cape St. Roque with ease. Captain Low says not enough masters trust Maury's charts yet. Low does wholeheartedly.

June 15. Latitude 1°28'S. Longitude 29°32'. Moderate breeze and cloudy. This morning crossed equator twenty-four days from New York. Children delighted with ceremony of welcoming Neptune on board and being "shaved" by him. Neptune played by sailor dressed in canvas robes, wig, and beard of rope. Razor was a barrel hoop; lather was grease laid on with a paintbrush.

At breakfast, Mrs. Low asked Captain if we might catch up with *Flying Cloud.* Captain changed subject - obviously hopes to do so but won't talk about it.

June 20. Latitude 16°11' Longitude 36°34'. Moderate breeze. Today is beginning of winter in southern hemisphere. We will round Cape Horn at worst time of year. Still pleasant weather here, temp. 80°. Cloudless sky turquoise blue. Ocean deep sapphire. Now almost a month out. Time passes quickly - reading, studying navigation, keeping journal, taking turns around the deck. In evening identify stars, sing, or just listen to sounds made by ship and wind and water. Idyllic.

Children always occupied. Help boys feed livestock. Pester carpenter or sailmaker, Hamilton Rea. Their favorite pastimes are whittling, learning to tie knots, listening to Rea's tales of sea and superstitions. Rea real old salt. Proud of the *Palmer.* Was sailmaker on *Horatio* with Captain Low when he shipped as a boy. Tells tales of Captain: how *Houqua,* his first command, on beam ends in hurricane. Low pulled her through and salvaged cargo.

June 25. Latitude 23°55' Longitude 42°20'. Moderate light breeze. "Land ho!" Most exciting sound at sea. At daylight, Cape Frio - east of

Rio - in sight, our first landfall. Now passing through variables of Capricorn, third area of Atlantic calms and variables.

June 27. Latitude 26°34' Longitude 45°12'. All week crew preparing *Palmer* for latitudes of the Roaring Forties and the Horn. Standing rigging carefully overhauled; new braces set up and rove off; heavy sails inspected, made ready for bending. Strongest sails needed for gales to come.

June 30. Latitude 31°30' Longitude 47°27'. Nippy breezes from Cape region, overnight weather change common in this area. Mate says we can now expect fights among crew. Does weather change have anything to do with mutinies? Today saw our first Cape pigeons - black heads, white bodies, mottled wings. They swoop gracefully around ship, or settle in water like ducks. Screechy, noisy, and ravenous. Will eat anything thrown overboard.

July 1. Latitude 32° 36' Longitude 48° 32'. Will soon be off Río de la Plata. Ship dressed in heaviest sails, prepared for pamperos, dangerous gales that roar out of 130-mile-wide river mouth. At noon ship sighted dead to windward. Captain took glasses to mizzen top for good look. Decided it was *Flying Cloud*. Much excitement. We are now hauled up close to wind with stun'sails shaking, waiting for her to come up.

July 2. Latitude 36°01' Longitude 50°51'. At 2:00 p.m.

yesterday spoke the *Flying Cloud.* Captain Low very proud at running up with her, beating her ten days so far and only forty days out. She is commanded by his old friend Captain Cressy. When *Cloud* came up alongside, Cressy hailed Low and wanted to know when we left New York. "Ten days after you," Low replied. Cressy so angry would say nothing more. *Cloud* at full speed ran ahead of us. Shortly after we filled away, wind pulled ahead. Had to brace sharp. Sent down skysail yards and royal stun'sail booms. Cloud has good start on us.

July 3. Latitude 39°36' Longitude 53°00'. Sighted *Cloud* 12 miles ahead, then lost her in mist. Captain says Mrs. Cressy on board. Always sails with husband - acts as his navigator. Today Mrs. Low's twentieth birthday. Steward baked cake. Good cake. Bad weather. Squally. Temp. 52°. Stove set up in main cabin.

July 8. Latitude 47°56' Longitude 54°13'. We are in the Roaring Forties. Stiff gales with snow, hail, and heavy head seas. Men constantly at pumps; shipping much water. Bitter cold. Can Cape Horn be worse than this?

July 9. Latitude 47°59' Longitude 56°27'. Now understand what Mr. Haines meant when he said change of weather might mean trouble. Last night, at midnight, there was mutiny. While making sail, sailor named Lemons shot Mr. Haines through leg. Another sailor, Dublin Jack, knocked second mate down with handspike. Captain Low, Mr. Haines, steward, carpenter, and sailmaker, all armed, went on deck with lantern. After crew had finished hoisting mizzen topsail, all hands ordered to pass in front of them, single file. Mr. Haines identified Dublin Jack as his attacker. Jack put in irons. Lemons came up, said *he* had done it. Captain asked where pistol was. "Overboard," said Lemons, adding that if it had been a revolver neither Captain nor mate would now be alive. Captain put Lemons in irons and ordered Jack released. Later discovered Jack had attacked second mate with handspike.

Captain had to show crew he was in command. Next morning called all hands to witness punishment. Had rope stretched across ship; with pistol in hand told men that if any stepped across rope he would shoot. Dublin Jack put one foot over. Captain went for him, caught him by throat, landed him on quarterdeck, put irons on him, and lashed him to mizzenmast. Lemons also triced to rigging. Captain ordered second mate to flog him. Mate refused, saying he had never done such a thing. Captain replied, "Neither have I," took rope and thrashed Lemons and then Dublin Jack, who were then put in booby hatch in irons.

Afterward Captain went forward. Told men if they were not satisfied with morning's work to step out one by one and he would thrash the whole lot. No one did. After breakfast, Captain worked all hands till no more mischief in them. Captain more than justified. Children bug-eyed with excitement. The lady passengers locked themselves in staterooms.

July 11. Latitude 51°45' Longitude 53°43'. Yesterday began to round Horn - from 50° S. Atlantic to 50° S. Pacific, about 1,200 miles, one of greatest tests of any sailing vessel. No further trouble with crew. Mr. Mowbray and Mr. Colby, the two British surgeons, are taking care of Mr. Haines. Report he will be laid up for some time. Ball went through thigh without breaking bone. There is much snow. Sailors shovel drifts overboard. Children make snowballs.

July 12. Latitude 53°23' Longitude 55°04'. Weather squally, light rain. Told children of great explorers who first sailed these latitudes - Magellan, Drake, Cavendish, Schouten, Cook. To west lies the strait through which Magellan reached Pacific. Strait separates mainland of South America from Tierra del Fuego - the "land of fires" of which Cape Horn is southernmost island. Latitudes bleak and cheerless. Climate damp. Winds cold, penetrating. Sun has no warmth, rises at 8:30, sets at 3:30. At noon today sun was still low on the horizon. Two hours later we had to light lamps.

July 15. Latitude 54°31' Longitude 61°12'. Hard to heavy gales for past two days, with heavy seas. Ship now prepared for the worst. Everything on deck lashed down. Shutters cover ports of deckhouses.

Life lines stretched fore and aft, for waves breaking over deck can sweep a whole watch away. Crew often in water to waist - call this their "daily soaking of corns."

Sail locker has been cleaned out and stove set up as "bogey room" where crew can dry clothes. At end of watch, each man allowed five minutes there to change clothes. Fo'c'sle never heated - change from wet cold to heat and back again would soon have every crew member sick.

Mr. Haines still laid up. Second and third mates incompetent, so whole burden falls on Captain Low. He is on deck day and night. We pray for quick and easy rounding.

July 16. Latitude 54°40' Longitude 62°56'. "Land ho!" As cry went up, children scrambled on deck. At 10:00 a.m. made Staten Land, bearing SSW twenty miles, first land seen since Cape Frio. Wild island, rugged, inhabited only by sea birds. We make southing under close-reefed topsails in gale from NNW.

July 17. Latitude 56°41' Longitude 66°00'. Now heading into Cape Horn rollers, mighty waves 1,000 feet from crest to crest that sweep unobstructed around the world. Rounding Horn in winter means fighting for westing against these seas, against gales laden with sleet and snow, against violent squalls. Hazard of icebergs always present.

Some ships have fought as long as ninety days to round Horn, clawing for westing, finally giving up. Yesterday passed large ship standing to SW. Could not identify. Was it *Flying Cloud*? Cape pigeons, albatrosses, petrels all about us.

July 18. Latitude 56°35' Longitude 68°00'. Fifty-seven days out. Cape Horn bearing N thirty-six miles. Climbed to mizzen top to see through drifting clouds this island first discovered and rounded by Schouten in 1616. Named for his Holland town of Hoorn. White squall blocked view. Sailmaker, describing violence of white squalls, tells of sailor who opened his mouth to speak in one. Wind blew him inside out. Nearing iceberg limits. Have doubled forward lookout. Running under double-reefed topsails and reefed courses.

July 19. Latitude 57°18' Longitude 69°30'. Cape Horn lives up to its nickname - Cape Stiff. Yesterday glass fell, wind began blowing from NNE with sleet, snow, and rain. Ocean terrifying. Heavy cross seas smoke with flying spume as giant waves collide.

Ship rolling badly. Lamps swing wildly on gimbals. Those with leeward bunks and windward seats at table lucky. Less danger of being tossed from bunk, or of food in lap. At supper last night, Mrs. Low, myself, and children only ones present. Ship gave great lurch. Steward baptized by bowl of stew. Children delighted. Steward philosophical.

Below in storm, one most aware of how flexible yet steely is the strength of a clipper. She seems alive as she yields to buffets of storm, complaining, shifting, and adjusting. If she had not been built well, of strong heavy timbers - white oak, live oak, locust, and cedar-sized and adjusted to meet the strains on her hull, she would pull herself apart.

Captain haggard, has lost much weight. On deck for ten days now, going below only to wind chronometers and take the time. He snatches sleep in corner of house on deck.

Crew magnificent. As gale winds higher, two men needed to control the wheel. "Close reef the topsails!" At the command, the men dart up ice-coated rigging. Sleet stabs, wind howls and claws at them. Aloft, on wildly swaying yardarms, they fist the frozen sails, beating the canvas, fighting for grip, their curses snatched away by the gale. How long does it take for just one reef? Eternity? Now back on deck, exhausted, huddled against lashing spray, waiting the next command to go aloft, looking forward to their watch below, hot coffee, a cold damp fo'c'sle, and a soggy bunk to rest on.

Through it all, an albatross soars serene and effortless into the gale. The sailors believe albatrosses are the souls of other sailors, drowned in these fierce seas. How they must envy and fear this great bird, riding the winds like a taunt!

Last night passed another hazard of Cape Horn - Diego Ramirez Rocks, jagged peaks thrusting straight out of the ocean. The Pacific lies ahead. Gale abating. Wind shifting to WNW. Ship rides more easily.

July 23. Latitude 54°44' Longitude 78°04'. Except for heavy snow squall from south, weather kinder. Made constant westing with stiff to moderate breezes. Now in Pacific sailing northward. Passengers, well bundled, able to get some air. Relieved that dread Cape is past, but Mr. Haines (still laid up) says bad weather may not be over. Tierra del Fuego to our east now. How comfortless are its place names - Famine Reach, Useless Bay, Deceit Rock, Desolation Island, Last Hope Inlet. Last night saw Southern Cross high above us. Stiff double-reefed topsail breeze.

July 29. Latitude 50°07' Longitude 77°47'. Five days of gales with rain, snow, and dangerous seas. Darkness seems endless. One night hove to under close-reefed main topsail. Next night, clapper of ship's bell got loose. Sounded as if tolling our doom. Weather worse than off Cape Horn. Captain and crew exhausted. But Captain now able to get some rest. After sixteen days, Mr. Haines again standing watch. Mrs. Low ideal captain's wife. Not once has she complained or shown fear. Most passengers have stayed in their berths. Not to sleep; just to keep warm. Today at noon weather calm, cloudy.

Sound of birds welcome. When by chance one lands on deck, his legs are so weak he cannot take off. He gets seasick. Children wanted to catch albatross with baited line. But sail-maker warned them of bad luck that would follow.

July 31. Latitude 49° 34' Longitude 79°00'. Have rounded the Horn. Twenty days. No way to beat the *Flying Cloud.* Now in Roaring Forties again. Glass falling. Gale expected.

August 7. Latitude 40°14' Longitude 77°30'. One solid week of gales. Winds ranged from forty to seventy miles an hour. But today barometer reads 30.1. First time over 30 since Latitude 45° in S. Atlantic. Moderate breeze. All sails set to best advantage. Ho! for California.

August 9. Latitude 37°34' Longitude 78°00'. Last night calm. First deep peaceful sleep for weeks. Captain tells us we head for Valparaiso to replenish supplies. Stupid stevedores stowed beef, bread, and coal under tons of cargo. Water also low. Now some 400 miles east of Juan Fernandez, Robinson Crusoe's island. Children plead with Captain to put in there for supplies.

August 17. At 7:00 p.m. anchored at Valparaiso in thirty-five fathoms. Weather for past week damp, foggy, unpleasant. Becalmed two days ten miles off shore.

August 21. Latitude 30°39' Longitude 73°42'. At

4:00 p.m. yesterday proceeded to sea with fine whole-sail breeze from SE and pleasant. At Valpo, mutineers taken off in custody of U.S. Consul. Will be sent home and tried for attempted murder on high seas. Twenty of our crew deserted but luckily replaced them with fine group of sailors who ship at high wages for short runs along Pacific coast. We are ninety-one days from New York. We drive, but not for records.

August 29. Latitude 15°10' Longitude 95°02'. Week of light and moderate trades. *Palmer* now wears light sails. Crew getting ship spick-and-span for port. Heavy Cape Horn storm sails mended and stowed. Slack on standing rigging from strains of heavy weather taken up, and rigging tarred - dirty job. Masts will be scraped and oiled, paint work scraped and painted, decks holystoned. Will arrive in San Francisco in newly beautiful ship - matter of pride for officers and crew of any vessel after long voyage. Have left albatrosses and Cape pigeons behind. Now accompanied by flying fish and noisy "bosun" birds - gull-size, white with scarlet beaks, croaking voices.

September 3. Latitude 4°27' Longitude 107°33'. We sail through whaling grounds. Children keep sharp lookout. Spotted only two huge turtles asleep on surface. They are carried by currents from Galápagos Islands. At 6:00 p.m. spoke whaleship *Rebecca Sims,* New Bedford. Her master, Captain

Parsons, reported he needed provisions. Both ships backed yards, Parsons came aboard. He is thirty-five months out. Anxious for news. We filled him in while crew did same for sailors who manned his boat. Gave us letters to mail. They left us in boat loaded with provisions, newspapers, books. As we squared away, his crew raised three cheers, ours sprang to rigging to answer with three, and his, as customary, gave one in return. After three years, how they must long for home! Temp. 70°. Brisk SE trades. All sails set.

September 11. Latitude 13°25'N. Longitude 122° 05'. Light airs and baffling, with some rain; 111 days out. After week of magnificent weather now in doldrums, losing SE trades which carried us well above equator. Crossed Line five days ago. Now on last leg of passage, and excitement of making port rises each day. Crew works with a will, painting and holystoning. Shanties ring out joyfully. Weather balmy. Ocean sparkles blue, and abounds with life - dolphins, sharks, schools of flying fish. Awning set up. Passengers on deck day and night. Have left Southern Cross. North Star with us again.

Sept. 21. Latitude 26°23' Longitude 135°58'. Only four days in doldrums. Now in NE trades. Yesterday weather glorious. At 2:00 p.m. made sail ahead. At 6:00 a.m. came up with and spoke our old friend *Gazelle,* last seen ninety-five days ago in the Atlantic. Her captain reported she was run into off Cape Horn by Spanish ship and had her bowsprit carried away, with all her head gear. She sails under jury rig.

September 27. Latitude 35° 37' Longitude 134°24'. Light breeze, flawy and baffling, overcast. Now in variables of Cancer, approximately 580 miles SW of San Francisco. NE trades have let go. Difficult to make northing and easting in this season. Finishing polish now being put on ship. Passengers packing. Crew probably making plans to desert and head for mines. Captain Low has had sharp watch put on sails to prevent stealing. (Stun'sails make good tents for miners.)

September 30. "Land ho!" At 7:00 a.m. made the Farallons. Everyone on deck to see these rocky islands twenty-five miles off Golden Gate that serve as pilot grounds. We have as a welcoming committee screeching gulls and barking seals, but no pilot boats. We head straight in, however.

Ship wears different look. Anchor catted; heaving lines, hawsers, buoys, and fenders placed alongside to be at hand when needed. We sail through Golden Gate, past Signal Hill, from which slatted arms of telegraph have already announced our coming, to magnificent San Francisco Bay. Harbor a jungle of vessels abandoned by forty-niners. Look in vain for *Flying Cloud.* Could we have beaten her?

Plagued by fleet of small boats manned by raucous boardinghouse runners. Surround ship like gulls, tossing packages of liquor and cigars to sailors, bragging, wheedling, each urging sailors to patronize *his* accommodations when their work is done. Everyone, including sailors, knows what will happen if they do. Will be plied with liquor, robbed, and probably shanghaied.

Flying Cloud has come and gone. She made port September 6, 113 days from New York. Sailed for China three days ago, runners tell us.

Crew, now bright with liquor, works ship as we head for Market Wharf. With crowds watching and as noon bells ring out, Captain Low hauls her up smartly alongside. Crowd cheers his seamanship. Crew quickly unbends fore-and-aft sails, stows them. Yards laid square, gaskets and ropes in neat condition, and the final order is given. "All hands pump ship!" Men race for the pumps. Wheels spin, plungers clank. Crew joyfully sings:

> I thought I heard the Old Man say,
>
> Leave her, Johnny, leave her!
>
> You can go ashore and draw your pay,
>
> It's time for us to leave her!
>
> Round and round they go as
>
> The winds were foul, the work was hard

Leave her, Johnny, leave her!

From the New York docks to the Frisco yard,

Leave her, Johnny, leave her!

Song floats across bay. Passengers and crews of other vessels line the rails to listen. This shanty signals the end of the run. Another clipper has fought its way around the Horn and made its way safely to port.

"'Vast heaving!" bawls the mate, and the work of the crew is done. With three loud cheers, the onlookers salute ship and crew alike. The *N. B. Palmer*, 130 days from New York, 125 days at sea, has arrived at San Francisco. All in all not too bad a run. Few ships that season did better.

5
TO THE LAND
DOWN UNDER

Gold! Once more the word sped around the world. In 1851, a man named Hargreaves, fresh from the California diggings, found gold in Australia. Again, the yellow metal exercised its magic, luring thousands from every continent to that distant land.

In the beginning, the gold was easier to find than in California. Indeed, it lay in the earth in quantities beyond belief. In a little more than a year after Hargreaves's discovery, $80 million worth had been taken from the diggings. Monstrous lumps containing as much as 100 pounds of pure gold were found. Such fabulous evidence accelerated the rush to the land "down under."

In the California rush, freight was carried by sailing vessels, while steamers transported the gold, the mails, and soon, most of the passengers. Australia, however, depended on sail for most of its transport - passengers, mail, gold, and goods alike. Only a few steamers made the run.

Shrewd American merchants - old hands now at gold rushes - began shipping goods to the British colony at once. The first clipper to sail, carrying gold seekers and freight, was the *Nightingale,* named for the "Swedish Nightingale," Jenny Lind, whose golden voice had recently enchanted America. In 1851, without benefit of Maury's charts, the *Nightingale* went out to Melbourne from New York in ninety days - then considered a fast run.

That same year, James Baines, an enterprising Englishman, started a new line of packets for Australia, calling it the Black Ball Line. While there was no connection between this Black Ball Line and the American one of the same name, Baines was accused of trying to trade on the splendid reputation of the American packets. Whether or not this was so, he took them as an example.

His first clipper for this line was the Canadian-built *Marco Polo.* Her accommodations for passengers, compared with those of other emigrant ships, were luxurious. She went out to Melbourne in 1852 on her maiden voyage under the command of Captain James N. Forbes in a record seventy-six-day passage, ran 438 miles in one day, and set a round-the-world mark of five months, twenty-one days. When she returned to Liverpool, a banner was strung between her fore and mainmasts proclaiming her "The Fastest Ship in the World." She became the model for speed and comfort on this run.

Matthew Maury had a hand in the speed of the *Marco Polo*. Before Maury began to chart the seas, ships sailing to Australia followed the same tracks out and back, rounding the Cape of Good Hope between latitudes 37° and 40°. The average passage each way was 120 days.

Maury advised outward-bound ships to keep some 600 to 800 miles clear of the African coast, head south as far as the latitudes of the Forties, and there pick up the "brave west winds" that blow with gale force unobstructed around the world. On the return passage, he advised continuing in the path of these same winds past Cape Horn and thence to England or the United States. Clippers following Maury's tracks around the globe found they were able to cut the time out and back nearly in half.

The Black Ball Line and its competitors, in the hope of acquiring other *Marco Polos,* had a number of ships built for them in Canada, but none of them came up to that clipper's mark. Nor did new English ships built for the trade. By 1853, it was clear that British shipping firms had but one place to turn for large, fast ships for Australia. That was the United States.

In June of 1853, the *Sovereign of the Seas*, with her builder, Donald McKay, aboard, ran from New York to Liverpool in a pace-setting thirteen days, nineteen hours. McKay's name was a familiar one in Liverpool, and the fame of his California clippers was widespread; now his *Sovereign of the Seas* had swept the seas. James Baines acted quickly. He chartered her for one voyage to Australia, and he contracted with McKay to build three big passenger packets for his Black Ball Line. These would be the *Lightning,* the *Champion of the Seas,* and the *James Baines.* (A fourth big ship, the *Donald McKay,* was ordered later.) McKay returned to Boston and went to work.

Baines advertised that he would return part of her freight money to shippers if the *Sovereign of the Seas* did not make a faster passage to Australia than any steamer. It was such an attractive offer that she carried a cargo valued at $1 million. But the "brave west winds" were elusive. Even as far south as latitude 53° her captain found no strong winds; he could go no farther south in search of them, for it was too cold for his insufficiently clothed crew. Notwithstanding the longish passage of seventy-seven days to Melbourne, Baines lost no money on his offer. The *Sovereign of the Seas* beat everything that had sailed against her, sail and steam alike.

Baines's principal rival, the White Star Line, also turned to American yards for ships. Their first was the *Red Jacket,* an extreme 2,305-ton clipper designed by Samuel Pook and built in Maine. Many considered her the most delicately beautiful of all the clippers.

The *Red Jacket* crossed from New York to Liverpool in thirteen days, one hour, snatching from the *Sovereign of the Seas* the crown for the shortest Atlantic passage from New York under sail. On her arrival, the White Star Line chartered her for one voyage to Australia. She was being made ready when the *Lightning,* the first of McKay's big clippers for James Baines, arrived at Liverpool from Boston, crossing in thirteen days, nineteen-and-one-half hours, and having on one of those days run 436 miles. Both clippers were scheduled to sail for Australia within a short time of each other.

Captain Samuel Reid of the *Red Jacket* knew he had an adversary in the *Lightning.* Even if he had not known, he would have found out from the *Lightning's* Captain Forbes, late of the *Marco Polo.*

Forbes was both a hard driver and a big talker. Before taking the *Marco Polo* out to Australia on her second voyage, he had announced: "Last trip I astonished the world with the sailing of this ship. This trip I intend to astonish God Almighty." If he did not, he certainly meant to keep on trying. His fighting slogan for the *Lightning's* maiden voyage was "Melbourne or hell in sixty days." When the *Lightning* sailed on May 14, 1854, ten days after the *Red Jacket,* he boasted that she would make Melbourne first and prove "the fastest ship in the world."

The *Red Jacket* ran her easting down to Melbourne pursued by winter gales and enveloped in the bitter cold of the high latitudes - "so cold that the ship was put down by the head by the frozen spindrift which covered her to the mainmast in an icy mantle." On one of these frigid days, she ran 400 miles. She survived her ordeal with the weather to make the shortest passage ever between England and Australia, sixty-seven days, thirteen hours. The *Lightning* took seventy-seven days to make the run; Captain Forbes swallowed his slogan.

On hand at Melbourne to greet Captain Reid and the *Red Jacket* was George Francis Train, the American-born Australian agent for the White Star Line. Train was a cocksure youngster of twenty-five, a nephew of the same Enoch Train who had earlier become McKay's patron. Arriving in Australia the year before, he set up the shipping and commission house of Caldwell & Train. He had energy, initiative, and enormous faith in his own capabilities and those of his fellow Americans. He later referred to himself as "Young America."

When he had arrived in Melbourne, Train was appalled by what he saw. He reported that the bay was filled with hundreds of vessels from all parts of the world, all waiting to be unloaded. There were no lighters, no wharves, no warehouses for goods. The more he saw, the angrier he got - no railway from the landing port to Melbourne, no merchants' exchange - no Yankee inventions of any kind! "All Melbourne requires to be a great city is a little energy and a great deal of money," he insisted. "We must introduce a sprinkling of Yankeeism. . . . Show the residents the meaning of dispatch."

In a little over a year, thanks in large measure to Yankee dispatch (there were 10,000 Americans in Australia), Melbourne was Americanized to Train's satisfaction. He had also shown the residents the meaning of Yankee shrewdness. Despite the glut of goods - enough to supply 5 million people had been shipped to a country whose total population was only 800,000 - Train, on well-chosen merchandise, realized profits of from 50 to 200 per cent. At the age of twenty-five, he was making $100,000 a year. By the time the *Red Jacket* arrived, Melbourne was in an excellent position for trade, and Train was one of its leading American citizens.

The day before the *Red Jacket* was to return to England, the *Nightingale,* newly chartered by the Australian Pioneer Line, arrived carrying 121 passengers, freight, and the mails. This line's clippers ran from New York to Melbourne, then to India or China for cargoes, often carrying teas and silks to England on their way back to New York. The

Nightingale had followed Maury's *Sailing Directions* this time and made the shortest run ever from New York - seventy-five days. But George Francis Train was much too busy to applaud the dispatch of a fellow countryman. There was a problem about the *Red Jacket's* sailing.

There were always problems connected with the sailing of a ship from Melbourne. The usual one involved crews. For clipper captains needing large crews, Melbourne, like San Francisco, was a madhouse. Seamen deserted for the diggings as soon as a ship made port, and captains had to settle for whatever could be rounded up for them. What they got, dumped on board drugged or drunk, was generally a mixed bag, ranging from able seamen to ex-convicts. (Captain Forbes, on his first passage in the *Marco Polo,* took care of this problem handily. He had his crew arrested on a trumped-up charge, thrown into jail, and put back aboard on sailing day.)

Train, however, faced a different problem with the *Red Jacket.* Because of a claim against the ship, Captain Reid was under arrest and could not sign the bill of lading for the $1 million worth of gold that Train, as agent for an English firm, was shipping to London. He wanted the clipper to sail on time, with the gold aboard. What to do? For Train, the solution was easy.

He signed for the captain, the gold was put on board, and the *Red Jacket* set sail. When the local bankers woke up to what Train had done, suspicion sprouted like beans on wet blotting paper. Train's partner was on board. Train's wife was on board. (She was returning to America to bear her child so that, if a boy, he would be eligible to become president.) Train himself was on board, and so was all that gold. Was it piracy? Was George Francis Train the reincarnation of Captain Kidd?

Two government men-of-war were sent out in pursuit of the clipper. In vain. The *Red Jacket* cleared the bay, a yacht put Captain Reid aboard - and took Train off. This confused the bankers but did not, however, convince them of Train's innocence. It might simply be part of the plot. Not until they learned of the *Red Jacket's* arrival in England would they relax.

Suspicions of piracy were natural enough, in the circumstances. Ships were sailing out from Australia on long passages to England laden with thousands of dollars worth of gold, and crewed in part by desperate, lawless men. The combination was potentially explosive.

In 1853, a passenger bound for England on board the *Medway* wrote that the ship carried four tons of gold dust stowed in boxes "under each of the berths of the saloon passengers. Each cabin was provided with cutlasses and pistols . . . and a brass carronade gun loaded with grape shot was fixed in the after part of the ship . . . pointed to the forecastle - not a man, with the exception of the ship's officers and stewards, being allowed to come aft."

Another ship sailing for England about the same time, also carrying four tons of gold dust, simply disappeared. It was supposed she had been seized by the crew, scuttled, and the gold taken off in boats. Homeward runs could be perilous passages.

As soon as Captain Reid boarded the *Red Jacket,* he realized that his clipper was not in good trim. In addition to the gold, she carried a poorly stowed cargo of wool, and she was too light for fast sailing. But Reid determined to make a run for it. Near Cape Horn, he found himself in an ice field, and for three days, with shortened sail, he dodged floes and bergs. For three nights, he could not sail at all. Nevertheless, he reached the equator in a speedy forty days. Then his luck changed. In the North Atlantic, he had nothing but head winds and calms. He was seventy-two-and-one-half days from Melbourne to Liverpool, no record, but an astonishing passage in light of sailing conditions.

Meanwhile, Captain Forbes in the *Lightning* was carrying on. Leaving Melbourne seventeen days after the *Red Jacket,* he found more favorable conditions than had Captain Reid - no ice off Cape Horn, no calms and headwinds in the North Atlantic. Vexed at having been beaten on the outward passage, Forbes drove his big ship day and night, and passengers told tales of his standing at the break of the poop with a pistol in his hand to prevent frightened sailors from letting the royal halyards go at the run.

The *Lightning* was sixty-three days from Melbourne to Liverpool. It was the shortest passage that would ever be made from Australia. She also rubbed out the *Red Jacket*'s newly-won round-the-world mark by two days, putting in its place her time of five months, eight days, twenty-one hours. Forbes was the cock of the Liverpool walk.

Meanwhile, the *Lightning*'s running mates, the *Champion of the Seas* and the *James Baines,* the second and third of McKay's big clippers for the British Black Ball Line, had arrived in Liverpool. (The *Donald McKay* would arrive the following year.) This remarkable quartet, although not sister ships, had many things in common: comfortable, well-ventilated quarters for steerage passengers; sumptuously decorated saloons, smoking rooms, and staterooms for cabin passengers. They were all heavily and strongly rigged. And from the maiden runs of each, it was clear they were all capable of great speed.

The *Lightning,* at 2,084 tons, was the smallest of the four. She had the sharpest and most concave entrance lines ever seen on a clipper. With little flare above these concavities to keep her buoyant and prevent her from burying, and a long deck amidships that caught and held water, she was a wet ship. Captain Anthony Enright took her over from Captain Forbes, made one voyage in her, and on his return recommended that the cavities be filled in. This was done, and her officers agreed that she sailed better and was drier. "Wood butchers of Liverpool!" growled Donald McKay. On her next voyage, the filling on one side washed away, the other was removed, and thereafter she sailed as modeled. Her fastest runs were made without these additions.

The *Champion of the Seas* was a three-deck clipper, as were the *James Baines* and the *Donald McKay*. She swung a main yard ninety-five feet long and could carry close to 13,000 running yards of canvas. She crossed from New York to Liverpool in a long passage of twenty-nine days, thereby proving nothing, for a sailing vessel can sail only if she has wind. It was said that time after time, her canvas yearned for just a cupful of breeze. She left Liverpool on her maiden voyage to Melbourne on October 12, 1854.

The clipper's passengers quickly settled down to amuse themselves as ship passengers do today. They played shuffleboard, quoits, or chess; they ran mimic horse races; they sat and read. Church services were held Thursday evenings and twice on Sundays, on the quarterdeck if the weather was fair. A weekly paper published news of the ship, of her run, and of her passengers - a baby was born, an elderly passenger died, another was lost overboard.

There seemed to be nothing out of the ordinary about the passage. It was, however, memorable. For between noon of December 11 and noon of December 12, 1854, while running in the latitudes of the Roaring Forties, with a heavy northwest gale blowing, the *Champion of the Seas* sailed 465 miles. It was the longest day's run ever made by any sailing vessel. In making it she proved herself truly the champion of the seas and reserved for herself a special place in the history of sail.

The *James Baines* (with a bust of James Baines, bewhiskered and top-hatted, as her figurehead) was very like the *Champion of the Seas* in design and rigging, the only difference being a slightly more raking stem. The English called her "the most perfect sailing ship that ever entered the River Mersey." She left on her maiden voyage to Australia on December 10, 1854, laden with a variety of livestock, 1,400 tons of cargo, and 702 passengers. She also carried 350 sacks of mail.

The White Star Line, after the *Red Jacket's* record passage to Melbourne, had signed a contract with the British government to deliver the mails to Australia in sixty-eight days or pay a penalty of £100 a day for each day over that figure. Thereupon the Black Ball Line contracted with the government to deliver the mails in sixty-five days or suffer the same penalty. It was up to the *James Baines* to make good the agreement.

In spite of poor sailing conditions in the Atlantic, the big clipper arrived at Melbourne in sixty-three days, having logged 407 miles in one twenty-four-hour period and 423 miles in another. George Francis Train reported that Melbourne "was fairly thrown on its beam ends" by her astonishing run, a run which no other clipper would ever duplicate. "Can anyone now doubt Donald McKay's supremacy on the ocean?" Train asked. No one could.

The *Donald McKay* was the largest of the quartet, 2,598 tons, and except for the *Great Republic,* the largest merchant ship afloat. Following Baines's instructions, McKay gave her much greater carrying capacity than the others, but she was still a sharp ship. She could carry more canvas than even the *Great Republic* - over 16,000 running yards - and she wore it with a difference, for her masts, instead of raking, were nearly upright. She was fitted with a new rig which enabled her crew to reef her topsails without going aloft.

The *Donald McKay* ran from Boston to Liverpool in February 1855, in seventeen days, on one of which, scudding before a hurricane, she logged 421 miles. On her maiden voyage to Australia, she was eighty-one days out and eighty-six days home.

All of the great one-day runs (400 miles and over) were made while sailing eastward driven by western winds. Four of them were made in North Atlantic gales. The others were made in the Roaring Forties. Here, ships running their easting down to Australia and home had 12,000 gale-ridden miles to log from the Cape of Good Hope to Cape Horn. And here, writes Carl Cutler, as the captains of the clippers strained to reduce their time, they "learned the trick of converting a heavy gale into a stiff breeze by merely continuing to run before it at eighteen knots or so."

Many a sailor preferred the trials of doubling Cape Horn to westward to running eastward in the Roaring Forties. "It's a terrible thing to have those greyhounds chasing you," a sailor said of the waves built up on the long rolling seas. It could be 12,000 miles of hell.

Take, for instance, a winter night, with the sky closed in, the air gray with blinding sleet and snow, the wind roaring wildly. A clipper, like a frightened deer pursued by baying hounds, scuds before the gale. Mountainous, frothing waves pursue her, threaten to overtake her, to smash her, to push her under.

A numb and ghostlike watch stands at the belaying pins ready to let go and clew up the sails at a moment's notice, for if the wind shifts a few points of the compass, the clipper can be taken aback, her masts sent crashing down. At times, the ship steers wildly. The helmsmen - two are needed now - strain to bring her back on course. The clipper leaps, startled, with each shift of the wheel. And always, with the greyhounds snarling at her heels, she hurtles forward, ever forward, a nightmare ship in a nightmare sea.

Driving before such gales was most dangerous for a slender light clipper, weighed down with cargo until her decks were only six feet above the water. Riding so low, she could be driven under or, with so little buoyancy, pushed under if too much water from the savage seas descended on her decks at once. For the crews of such clippers, laboring almost in the sea itself, it was a nightmare, indeed.

On the other hand, McKay's big Australian clippers, flat-floored, long, and heavy, were ideally suited to driving in these latitudes. Carrying passengers instead of cargo, they sailed in better trim, having as much as fifteen feet of freeboard and, therefore, less of their hull in the water. Because they were higher and drier, their crews had a better time of it. But for any crew on any ship, the Roaring Forties could be an interesting experience.

In 1857, the British government chartered the *Lightning,* the *James Baines,* and the *Champion of the Seas* to carry troops to India to quell the Sepoy Mutiny. As the *Baines* and the *Champion of the Seas* lay at Portsmouth, their fame reached Queen Victoria herself, who requested that they not sail until she had paid them a visit. After being conducted over the *James Baines,* she expressed her pleasure "that so splendid a merchant ship belonged to her dominions."

These two clippers, each carrying about 1,000 soldiers, sailed for Calcutta on the same day and arrived together, 101 days out. While regimental bands on board tooted and soldiers cheered wildly, they raced in on a three-skysail breeze. It was an unforgettable moment.

Meanwhile, American clippers had been busily plying between England and Australia, and the United States and Australia. One of the clippers chartered by the Australian Pioneer Line was the little 776-ton *Mandarin,* built in 1850 for the California trade. Almost flat-floored, with sides nearly straight, she was well suited to driving in heavy weather. In 1856, she sailed from New York to Melbourne in sixty-nine days, fourteen hours, the fastest time that would ever be made between these ports by a sailing ship.

Matthew Maury estimated that New York was, in sailing time, ten days farther from Melbourne than were English ports. Ships sailing from England had the benefit of the northeast trades on the first part of the voyage; those from American ports did not. Taking Maury's estimate into account, the sixty-nine-day run from New York of the six-year-old *Mandarin* stands up proudly next to the sixty-three-day record from Liverpool of the *James Baines* - a new ship more than three times her size.

In the spring of 1858, the *James Baines,* with a cargo of Indian goods, returned to Liverpool in seventy-seven days - the record from Calcutta. It was the last run the big ship would make, for she was destroyed by fire a week later. So the "noblest ship of the Black Ball fleet" ended her days as she had begun, by setting a record. On her remains was built the Liverpool Landing Stage, used by passengers debarking from Atlantic steamers.

The *Donald McKay,* the fourth McKay ship built for the Black Ball Line, was the last clipper constructed in the United States at the order of an English firm. For some time, there had been rumbles in England over the amount of business going to American instead of British shipyards. James Baines was even accused of being anti-British. To pacify public opinion, Baines ordered from James Hall, of Aberdeen, Scotland, an enormous emigrant clipper of 2,600 tons named the *Schomberg.* She was the largest wooden sailing ship ever built in Britain, and Baines gave her command to Captain Forbes.

Extravagant claims were made for the *Schomberg:* She would out-sail and outlast any clipper built by the Yankees; she was the ship that would unseat America and put England back in her traditional place as ruler of the waves. Forbes, pointing to a sign in her rigging that read "Melbourne in 60 Days," said modestly, "I expect to do better than that." Her sailing was made a patriotic occasion, and the hopes of Britain sailed with her.

Forbes drove her for all she was worth, but when he realized her passage would be closer to eighty than sixty days, he sulked and lost interest. He was playing whist when Australia was sighted. He played on. The mate reported the ship too close to shore. He played another rubber before coming on deck. By then, it was too late. The *Schomberg* grounded on a sandbank. Forbes quit his ship in a boat, and in a short time, the *Schomberg* was pounded to pieces by the sea. England never again tried to build a big clipper.

During the later part of the 1850s, the Peninsular & Oriental Steam Navigation Company extended its line from Suez to Australia and began to give clippers serious competition. England built iron sailing vessels for the trade, vessels capable of carrying large cargoes as well as passengers.

Nevertheless, the American-built clippers continued to give good and faithful service on the run. McKay's big ships served over thirteen years, the *Red Jacket* close to ten. But none ever lived up to Forbes's slogan and made Melbourne in sixty days.

6
TWILIGHT

As far as speed was concerned, the year 1854 began auspiciously for the clippers. In March, the name of the clipper *Comet* was set down in the records as having made the shortest run from San Francisco to New York - seventy-six days, seven hours. And in April, Josiah Cressy and the *Flying Cloud* shaved thirteen hours off their own record to California, making the passage in eighty-nine days, eight hours.

But these were the only highlights in the picture. The California trade was slowing down, and the boom in the shipping industry was turning into bust. The bright speculative years were over. By fall, eastern harbors were crowded with ships waiting for charters - 777 idled in New York harbor alone.

Only 111 clippers sailed for California that year; only sixty-nine clippers came off the stocks. Six of these were extreme, the last extreme clippers ever to be launched.

In New York shipyards, where once the air had been filled with the smell of fresh sawdust, the sound of hammers, and the rasp of saws, there was, in 1855, an ominous quiet. Nevertheless, all was not bleak. There were a few heartening developments.

California began shipping wheat to Atlantic ports, providing a return cargo for the clipper ships. Then England and France, at war with Russia in the Crimea, chartered a number of clippers as troop transports.

One of these was the newly rebuilt *Great Republic.* Lying in the Thames at London - no dock was large enough to accommodate her - she created a sensation because of her size. Her captain reported that visitors asked "whether he had left any lumber for shipbuilding in the United States, or brought it all with him."

The China-to-England tea trade picked up. Twenty-four American ships loaded tea for England, more than during any previous year. The words of the shanty, "Flying fish sailor, ninety days from Hong Kong," could well have applied to a member of the crew of the *Nightingale.* She made the record run of ninety days, eighteen hours, from Shanghai to London.

There was also one glorious day in August 1855, when seven clippers sailed through the Golden Gate, folded their wings, and came to rest in San Francisco Bay. Never had any port seen such a breathtaking sight. None would ever see it again.

And from the shipyard of Irons & Grinnell, in the little port of Mystic, Connecticut, the 1,679-ton *Andrew Jackson,* a heavily-sparred medium clipper, was launched.

In spite of the fact that the market was now apparently glutted with some 340 clippers, in 1855, thirty-five more slid down the ways. But, like the *Andrew Jackson,* they were medium clippers - a new type.

Extreme clippers were expensive to build, expensive to operate, and expensive to repair. Moreover, they could carry comparatively little cargo for their tonnage. When freight rates began tumbling - to $28 a ton in 1854, from a high of $60 in 1850 - the owners of these sharp ships faced a profit squeeze. And so, the medium clipper was developed, a ship at once fast and yet able to carry nearly double her registered tonnage and so earn more money per voyage than her older, sharper sisters.

The relief that 1855 brought to the shipping industry was only temporary. In the spring of 1856, the war in the Crimea ended, and the clippers that saw service under French and English flags were once more at liberty. English competition was increasing in the tea trade - she was building up her own fleet of small, swift tea clippers. Too many ships had been built. There was simply not enough trade to keep them busy. More and more clippers had to turn to the detestable Asian worker and guano trades.

Guano, used as a fertilizer, is found on the Chinchas, three barren, rocky islets a dozen miles off the coast of Peru. Here, over the centuries, millions of sea birds and seals lived and died, forming with their excrement and remains round hills of guano, in some places over 150 feet deep. Ships came from all over the world to carry it back to their homelands. In the 1850s, there were always scores of them at anchor, often waiting two or three months for their turn to be loaded.

The guano trade was debasing and degrading to the captains and to their clippers. To the Asians who dug the stuff, it was death.

The Asian workers had come from China to labor for the Peruvian government for a period of five years. Decent working conditions were promised them; instead, they were housed in rude cane huts, grossly underfed, and given only rags to wear. They were worked by brutal overseers from sunrise to sunset, seven days a week. Those who did not die from starvation, exhaustion, or breathing guano dust committed suicide by jumping from the cliffs into the sea. As fast as they died, they were replaced by others.

For captains forced to wait months to take on their cargoes, there was nothing but boredom and helpless fury. To pass the time and possibly to try to forget man's inhumanity to man, they organized balls, regattas, picnics, and boating excursions. When at last it came a clipper's turn to be loaded, she was drawn up close to a cliff. The Asian workers, their mouths and noses covered with thick bandages, shoveled the guano into sleeve-like chutes that led directly into the ship's hold. All the while, the vessel was enveloped in a cloud of yellow, reeking guano dust that penetrated everywhere, tarnishing brass and silver and covering all with its pollution.

With her foul cargo finally on board, the clipper's flag was hoisted, and her crew gave three cheers, which were answered by the crews of all the other vessels at anchor. At last, she was free of the islands, but not of the guano dust. It usually took a week at sea to get a ship clean, and the upper spars and tackle stayed yellow until she got into the rainy weather off Patagonia. The memory of the murderous slavery on the Chinchas could never be so easily washed away.

The worst use to which the clippers were put was the transporting of the Asian workers from China to the Chinchas, or to Australia and Cuba. English vessels had long been in this profitable business.

By the 1850s, ship owners were getting from $50 to $80 for each Asian they carried. This meant that a shipload of 800 was worth at least $40,000.

And so, when charters became scarce, American clippers began competing with British ships for this shameful trade. In 1856, the *Winged Racer* and Donald McKay's *Westward Ho* brought 1,500 Asian workers to Peru. But their flogging by the captain of the *Winged Racer* aroused public opinion, and the owners were forced to forego the fat profits of the trade. Not entirely, however, for they sold the *Westward Ho* to the Peruvian government, which continued to sail her in the reprehensible trade. By 1857, the great powers, forced by public opinion to condemn the atrocities in the Chinchas, forbade ships flying their flags to transport Asian workers to Peru. Peru simply bought more American clippers.

Moreover, American clippers continued to transport Asian workers to Cuba and Australia. Boatloads of them were literally kidnapped, and during the passage, they were treated less decently than cattle. On one ship, there were floggings, suicides, and finally mutiny, with the Asians trying to set the ship on fire. By the time the vessel arrived at Havana, 130 Asian laborers had perished - seventy killed when the mutiny was suppressed, the others dead of dysentery.

This loathsome trade even claimed the lovely *Sea Witch*. In 1856, with a cargo of 500 Asian workers on board, she piled up on a reef a few miles from Havana, a sad and bitter end for one of the greatest of all the clippers.

That winter the weather off the Horn was especially hard. In bitter cold, Captain Phineas Winsor in the *Rapid* bucked gales and hurricanes for week after week. One by one his sails went; one by one his crew went, dead or lying injured in the fo'c'sle. Finally, with ten seamen dead, ten helpless, and only four left to limp about, he reluctantly turned back to Rio - the only time a clipper sound in masts and hull turned back from the challenge of the Horn.

Off the Horn at the same time, another battle was being fought on board another clipper, the extreme *Neptune's Car.* Her captain, Joshua Patten, was in his cabin, deaf and blind, sick with brain fever. His first officer was under arrest for insubordination, and the captain's wife, nineteen-year-old Mary Patten, was in command. She had learned navigation on a previous voyage, and with the help of an illiterate but faithful second mate, she fought the big clipper round the Horn and brought her safely to San Francisco, caring for her husband all the while. Mary Patten was hailed as the Florence Nightingale of the ocean.

Such courage was typical of the "old women" who sailed the clippers with their "old men." (To a sailor the captain's wife was the "old woman" and the captain the "old man," no matter what their ages.) They were as brave and resourceful as their husbands, and their presence on board added a gentling touch to the hard life of the sea.

The financial panic of 1857 dealt the clippers a fearsome blow. Not only the clippers but the country as a whole had run out of the wind and was becalmed, sails slatting. Only six clippers came off the stocks. The end was clearly in sight. The *Twilight,* a medium clipper built at Mystic, was one of the last, and her name was prophetic. Donald McKay closed his yard to wait for better times. Many yards closed forever.

In the California trade, with freight rates at rock bottom - $10 a ton - only sixty-eight clippers sailed. In the China-to-England tea trade, American clippers found it more and more difficult to get charters. Many of the older clippers - most of them cut down and overhauled for safety as well as for economy - were to lie idle for two or more years. Even the magnificent *Flying Cloud* was laid up.

America, which a few brief years before had been at the very peak of her powers as a maritime nation, whose ships had swept the seas as none had ever done before, was headed down the long trail of nautical decline.

On October 10, 1858, San Francisco's streets echoed to the clatter of the first transcontinental stagecoach, twenty-three days, twenty-three-and-a-half hours, from St. Louis. Where once San Francisco had given an ovation to the arrival of a record-breaking clipper ship, now the cheers greeted the arrival of another, swifter kind of transportation.

The overland stage epitomized a vast change of national attitude. Where previously ships and shipping had attracted the brightest and most energetic minds of the country, now the challenge was to open and develop the West. People were no longer interested in the sea as a career. It was too hard, too risky a life.

The year 1858 seemed to underscore the hardships and the risks. In January, the *John Gilpin* struck an iceberg and was abandoned off the Horn; all hands were saved by a British ship. In February, the *John Milton* was driven ashore near Montauk, Long Island, in a bitter snowstorm, and all hands were lost. The same month, the *Flying Dutchman* was lost on Brigantine Beach, New Jersey. In March, the *Wild Wave* went up on a coral island not far from Pitcairn Island in the Pacific; all hands were presumed lost. Later that year the *Flying Fish,* coming out of Foochow with tea for New York, was wrecked in the turbulent "chow-chow" waters of the Min.

By this time, many of the men who had ushered in the era of the clipper ships had left the sea. Nat Palmer was retired, content to sail his yacht and do a little fishing. Robert Waterman was the port warden at San Francisco. Josiah Cressy and his wife left the *Flying Cloud* and retired to a quiet life in the old Massachusetts seaport of Salem.

Philip Dumaresq, often called "the Prince of Sea Captains," almost saw the era out, not retiring until 1859, after slamming the medium clipper *Florence* from China to England. He was then fifty-five years old, twice as old as most sea captains, but he still drove his ship and himself as mercilessly as ever.

To the captains who still sailed the seas in clippers, the events of these years, discouraging and disheartening as they were, mattered little. Freight rates might be low. Speed might not be so important anymore. But old or new, extreme or medium, cut down or sailing under her first full spread of canvas, a clipper was still a clipper. And there was only one way to sail her - to drive her for all she was worth. There might be no more neck-and-neck races round the Horn, but there was always a mark to shoot at - for instance, that of the *Flying Cloud.*

In November of 1859, after being laid up for over two years, the *Flying Cloud* was sold. Faded now and weather-beaten, she was taken to a repair yard to have her spars cut down and her sail-spread reduced so that a small economy crew could handle her. While being towed up the East River, she passed Pier 20 from which she had twice sailed to glory. She also passed the *Andrew Jackson* lying at her wharf, "up for California." Along the riverfront a few old salts watched the *Cloud* being towed along, remembered, and were saddened.

On Christmas Day, when Captain Jack Williams sailed in the *Andrew Jackson* for California, he needed no recent glimpse of the *Flying Cloud* to spur him on. He and his clipper had raced a phantom *Flying Cloud* on three previous passages to San Francisco. Two they made in 100 days, one in 103. They still raced her.

The log of the *Andrew Jackson,* written in Captain Williams's own hand, gives a delightful picture of a mariner with a sound sense of what was important. His time, compared to that of the *Flying Cloud,* was what mattered; spelling did not.

He crossed the equator on January 14 in "Twenty Days & Twelve houers." (The *Flying Cloud* had done so in seventeen days.) The next day, finding himself far west, he noted: "It look Kind a hard for Cap St. Rook this time," but he rounded the Cape without too much difficulty, reaching Latitude 50° S in "Forty-Three and a Hafft Days" to the *Flying Cloud's* forty-two. On the way, he observed "a Large Curkel Round the Sun," and "A Mackrel Sky and Mears Teiles & Read in the Morning."

For four days, after passing the Horn, the clipper had rough going with heavy squalls and bad seas. But she reached Latitude 50°S in the Pacific

"Fifty-Three and Hafft Days" out, twelve hours ahead of the *Cloud.* Captain Williams noted with satisfaction, "The Barometer is going up Nicely and I am in hope to havey a good run Yeat."

Recrossing the equator, seventy-three days out, he was a full day ahead of the *Cloud,* and his time, he recorded proudly, was the "Shortest but Three on Record."

For the first eighty-two days of his voyage, Captain Williams was like a small boy who crosses his fingers for luck. It was as though even to mention the *Flying Cloud* in his log might put a hex on his chance of trimming her record. But on the eighty-third day, his confidence was high; for the first time he set down the name of his ghostly adversary and confessed, "I am in hopes yeat to Do as well as the *Flying Cloud's* time."

But three days later, the winds were "Baffling and Puffey." He was getting anxious: "I am in hopes the wind will come to the west Soone." But not for two long days would his prayer be answered. Then up it came strong and squally, speeding him along. The next day, March 22, 1860, with one more day to go, he wrote, "We are good for the *Flying Cloud* Yeat." And he was. At 4:00 p.m. the following afternoon, he "made the Farallons . . . eighty-nine days and houers from New York." The *Andrew Jackson* had snatched the crown, shaving four hours from the record run.

Captain Williams was unable to get a pilot until the following morning, and for that reason, the actual port-to- port time of the *Flying Cloud* is shorter than that of the *Andrew Jackson*. But it is sailing time that is important, and San Franciscans had no doubts about the run of the *Andrew Jackson*. They gave Captain Williams an ovation, presented him with a commodore's pennant for the shortest passage ever made from New York to San Francisco, and wanted to parade him around town in a carriage. But Jack Williams was too modest a man to accept. He was content to have his name go down in the record book as the captain of the clipper that had made the fastest sailing passage ever around Cape Horn.

When the *Andrew Jackson* returned to New York, she crossed to Liverpool in fifteen days and returned "uphill" in another fifteen days. Her westward passage and her round trip of thirty days set records.

These runs of the *Andrew Jackson* provided a fitting flourish to the golden years of the clipper ships. They ended as they had begun, with a record smashed, and a new name written on the scroll of the sea.

7
END OF THE ERA

In the age of steam, there suddenly had been a need for swift ships - in the China trade, the California trade, the Australian trade. Steamships were in their infancy; they were dangerous, expensive to operate, and slow. It was up to the wind ships to do the job. With only the tools of vanished centuries at hand - canvas and hemp and wood - men were challenged to meet the demands of a new epoch, to make a heroic effort to harness the winds, to build ships that would sail faster than any other vessels in the history of sail.

They succeeded gloriously. For a few brief years, the clippers swept the seas. Then, when they were no longer needed, they ceased to be. But before that time, thousands had quickened to the excitement of the challenge.

The building of the clippers was not the work of a few shipbuilders in a few seaports. Donald McKay at Boston and William Webb at New York turned out a greater number of clippers than did any other yards. But scores of workers, carpenters, sail-makers, sparmakers, riggers, and others, in shipyards from Maine to Florida, knew the pride of making a clipper ship grow.

And, once she was built, still others strove to make her rise to the challenge. Scores of captains and officers took on the responsibility. They drove themselves, they drove their ships, and they drove the sailors of all nationalities who sailed under them. And together they made the dream become a reality.

In this quest for speed, there was always something to be changed, some improvement to be made. "I never yet built a vessel that came up to my own ideal," Donald McKay said. "I saw something in each ship which I desired to improve." The legend persists that Samuel Pook, one of the first naval architects, worked in close collaboration with McKay. But whether he did or not, in this search for perfection, certainly Pook's ideas, as well as those of Nat Palmer and John Griffiths, went into the creation not only of McKay's ships but of all the clippers. So did the ideas of many others, shipmasters, shipbuilders, and designers alike.

Before the clipper ship era was over, all of the basic mysteries of fast-sailing design had been unfolded. Indeed, the lines of the ocean greyhounds of today owe more than a little to those people who worked more than a century ago.

There are many ways of judging the speed of a ship: by knots per hour, by day's runs, by port-to-port records. Judged by any test, the American clippers were supreme.

Donald McKay's *Sovereign of the Seas* reported the highest rate of speed – twenty-two knots, made while running her easting down to Australia in 1854. (John Griffiths' first clipper, the *Rainbow,* had a top speed of fourteen knots.) There were eleven other instances of a ship's logging eighteen knots or over. Ten of these were recorded by American clippers, the other by the Canadian-built *Marco Polo.*

Besides the breath-taking 465-mile day's run of the *Champion of the Seas,* there are thirteen other cases of a ship's sailing over 400 nautical miles in twenty-four hours. Again the *Marco Polo* is the only non-American clipper listed.

And with few exceptions, all the port-to-port sailing records are held by the American clippers.

There is no single clipper that one can point to and say, this was the fastest. Some were built to speed along in one kind of weather, others to speed along in another. Still others, like the *Flying Cloud,* were built for general weather conditions.

On the California run, there was no foreign competition (this was considered a coasting run; foreign competition was not allowed), and the clippers fought it out among themselves. Matthew Maury estimated that under optimum conditions, the fastest sailing time that could ever be made from New York to San Francisco was eighty-five days. No sailing ship ever found those conditions. Of nearly 1,000 clipper passages made between 1849 and 1860, only twenty times was the 15,000-mile run made in under 100 days.

The smallest ship to break the mark was the 900-ton *Sea Witch;* the largest, the 3,357-ton *Great Republic.* The *Sea Witch* had hollow bows and a V-shaped bottom, most practical for the China run on which a ship needed to be able to ghost along in light, variable airs, and she holds the records from Canton and Hong Kong to New York. The *Great Republic,* on the other hand, was long and comparatively flat-floored. She had been built specifically for the Australian run, where a ship needed strength and weight to hold her to her course. Yet both of these ships, so far apart in size and design, came close to the record time on the California run. As with all ships that sailed this racecourse, if one had an advantage in light airs, another might have it in heavy weather off the Horn.

Most of a clipper's best runs were made in her early years. Five or six years of hard driving strained and weakened her, and she could not be pushed so hard. Moreover, being made of wood, she absorbed water and thus became sluggish in light airs. There were, however, always exceptions. The *Swordfish* (dubbed "The Diving Bell" by some of her crews because of her tendency to bury when driven) set the record from Shanghai to New York - eighty-one days - when she was nine years old.

Beauty has been defined as having two requirements - first, that the object or thing be fit for its purpose in all its parts, and second, that it have perfect proportions and colors in a well-balanced harmony.

There can be no doubt that the clippers were fit for their purpose - to carry cargo swiftly. They were also a delight to the eye. Their hulls were painted black (some carried stripes of gold, red and white, or crimson); their yards and bowsprits were usually black; their lower masts usually white to the tops; the tops and doublings above were scraped bright and varnished. The only touch of fancy was in their names and figureheads. Those who were lucky enough to see a clipper sailing before a fair wind on a crisp sunny day, her soaring masts splendid with snow-white sail, water creaming past black bows, saw perfect proportions and colors in a well-balanced harmony. Fit for her purpose from truck to keel, from taffrail to jib boom, the clipper ship was beautiful, indeed.

But her beauty and her days of glory were fleeting. Soon the sleek, lean race horse turned drab, working at menial, degrading tasks.

The years of the Civil War brought many changes to the clipper fleet. Some became cruisers in the U.S. Navy. Others were captured and burned by Confederate raiders. Still others were laid up to escape capture or destruction.

During this period, England changed her policy about foreign-built ships, and British firms leaped at the chance to pick up American clippers at bargain prices. Flying the house flags of the White Star Line and James Baines's Black Ball Line, many of them, including the *Flying Cloud,* were to see years of service on the Australian run. Peru bought four more clippers for the Asian worker trade. And a number of others were lost - to fire, to collision at sea, or to typhoons. The *Andrew Jackson* piled up on a reef in the East Indies, a total loss. The *Lightning* burned in Melbourne harbor.

The *N.B. Palmer,* Charles Low on her quarterdeck, continued to ply between China and New York. "The old ship is as staunch and strong as the day she was built," Low wrote his wife. "I am so infatuated with this exciting life I do not know how I can ever give it up." Low finally retired from the sea in 1873, and his beloved *N.B. Palmer,* "Queen of the China clippers," was sold abroad. Two clippers continued in the California trade until as late as 1883, faded beauties but still driving.

Sold and resold, cut down again and again, sailing under different names as if ashamed of themselves, the clippers went from one dismal job to another. They carried coal, case oil, lumber, and guano; the speed for which they had been so perfectly designed was no longer needed.

The *Flying Cloud* and the *Red Jacket* turned up as lumber droghers in the North Atlantic trade. When the *Cloud* went ashore at St. Johns in 1874, she was burned for the copper and iron in her hull. The *Red Jacket,* no longer useful even for this dull job, finally ended her days as a coal hulk. The *Donald McKay* met the same fate. The *N.B. Palmer* and the *Nightingale* sailed on under the Norwegian flag. One ferried case oil, the other lumber. Both were abandoned in the North Atlantic in the early 1890s.

On January 3, 1877, the *Champion of the Seas,* Captain Wilson, en route to Cork with a cargo of guano, was abandoned in sinking condition in the North Atlantic. She had sprung a leak, and her pumps had choked. Her officers and crew were taken off by a bark, *the Windsor.* The two captains watched as the gallant old clipper, one of the swiftest that ever sailed the seas, settled slowly in the water.

Suddenly the *Windsor's* captain noticed something on the poop of the sinking clipper. "Captain," he said, "you have left one of your men on board!" Captain Wilson took up his glasses, looked, smiled, and explained. It was only a life-sized figure of a sailor boy, holding in his hands the binnacle, the housing for the compass that pointed the way. There was no need for concern. There was no one on board. What was going down was only an image, a symbol of an already vanished era.

Many sailing ships came after the clippers - small British tea flyers, grain ships, wool ships, nitrate ships. Many were good ships, brave ships, hard-driven ships. Yet none ever captured hearts as did the clippers.

They are gone now. There is not one American clipper left in the world today. And yet their glories will never die. They will sail on forever in the hearts of all those who love beauty, of all those who thrill to a challenge braved and won.

SOURCES

Robert G. Albion, *Square-Riggers on Schedule (Princeton, New Jersey:* Princeton, 1938).

Ralph K. Andrist, *The California Gold Rush* (Boston, Massachusetts: New Word City, 2015).

Helen Augur, *Tall Ships to Cathay* (New York, New York: Doubleday, 1951).

Robert Carse, *The Moonrakers* (New York, New York: Harper, 1961).

Chapelle, Howard I. *History of American Sailing Ships* (Boston, Massachusetts: Houghton Mifflin, 1959).

Arthur Clark, *The Clipper Ship Era* (New York, New York: G. P. Putnam Sons, 1911).

Richard H. Dana, *Two Years Before the Mast* (New York, New York: Dodd, Mead, 1946).

Basil Lubbock, *The Romance of the Clipper Ships* (New York, New York: Macmillan, 1959).

John R. Spears, *Captain Nathaniel Brown Palmer* (New York, New York: Macmillan, 1922).

Edward A. Stackpole, *Great Adventures of the Sea* (New York, New York: Dial, 1961).

Alan Villiers, *The Way of a Ship* (New York, New York: Scribner's, 1953).

Printed in Great Britain
by Amazon